Freedom In Every Moment

Transcending the Struggles of Daily Life

Vincent J. Morello, Ph.D.

AND

David F. O'Connell, Ph.D.

Published by Motivational Press, Inc.
1777 Aurora Road
Melbourne, Florida, 32935
www.MotivationalPress.com

Manufactured in the United States of America.

ISBN: 978-1-62865-358-8

CONTENTS

PREFACE

• • • • •

We have choices in life, many of them. In fact, there is a choice in each and every moment of our lives. We can choose to pay attention to what we think or feel, which, at times, is uplifting, and, at other times, not. Or, we can choose something else. This book is for those of us who wish to choose something else, something greater, our own Inner Divinity.

Freedom from the shackles of our inner worlds, our thoughts and our feelings, is as close as our breath, if we choose to attend to it. We can experience freedom in each and every moment if we like. We can be free from worry, what others think, and from our dark moods. If we do not like the status quo of our inner lives, we do not have to accept it.

There are many people on this earth who walk about in complete freedom in each and every moment, and they have given us great guidance as to how we can live in the same state, just as gingerbread crumbs have been placed on the ground for us to follow the trail home. Why not follow their guidance, their suggestions? They would so much like us to join them in freedom.

This volume contains some of the guidance from the great Masters, imploring us to seek our freedom. The guidance is in the form of a journey, starting from who we think we are to who we truly are. Free persons...in each and every moment.

INTRODUCTION

• • • • •

Since your early childhood years, you likely have spent less and less time living in the present moment. By virtue of living on this earth, you have been systematically trained to worry about the future (anxiety) or regret what you have done in the past (depression). Most of us do not fully experience everyday life, but instead 'live' in the world of our thoughts, and often feel overcome by them. We have been led to believe there is no other way to live. We have also been led to believe that by worrying about the future and regretting our actions in the past, we are doing the right thing! The more we worry, the more we believe we are responsible people, handling situations as mature adults and keeping a lid on things. Truthfully speaking, in short, this is the problem in having a mind.

In addition to our challenging inner mental circumstances, living a low- stress life appears, day by day, to be more and more of an effort. As practicing psychologists, we observe increasing stress in our own lives as well as those of the patients coming to our psychology offices, who complain of anxiety or work/family stress. Concerns about terror attacks, financial difficulties, and an adequate number of decent paying jobs fill our newspapers and websites. A 'Psychology of Fear' is being ingrained in the mass consciousness of the United States, as well as in countries all over the globe. Recent data from the National Center for Health

Statistics shows a 24% increase in the suicide rate in the United States from 1999-2014. This increase was evident in all age groups, and particularly among women and middle-aged Americans, aged 43-64 years—groups that traditionally showed lower relative rates. Social isolation, financial concerns, and joblessness were implicated as possible causal factors for this increase.

There is virtually no avoiding exposure to stress, unless one is on vacation. When we were children, it was fairly common for many middle-class families to take a two-week vacation every summer. Now, most working Americans take fewer days off for vacation than our predecessors did a mere 50 years ago, making it ever more difficult to get a break from the daily grind. Many people are lucky to get five consecutive days off from work for a weeklong vacation. Moreover, patients frequently inform us that when they are on vacation, they often are required to respond to work Emails, regardless of whether it is morning, noon, or night. This trend of being on call at work 24/7 is likely to continue, which will increase the stress load for many employees. Sadly, vacation is no longer the antidote for stress it once was.

Given this somewhat bleak state of affairs, it would be only natural to wonder whether we are doomed to lifetimes of high stress levels, no matter what our outer circumstances are. It may be ridiculous to imagine having the kind of lower-stress lifestyles enjoyed by our parents' and grandparents' generations. Yet the good news is that it is definitely possible to live a life containing far less stress than you have right now.

In fact, throughout the centuries, there have always been persons living among us who are completely untouched by stress. These individuals are called by various names, such as

Great Beings, Saints, and Sages. Regardless of life circumstances, they have lived in states of peace, contentment, and bliss. They exist, and have existed, in all cultures. Some are followers of particular religions, while some do not adhere to any particular religion. More importantly, many have a mission to serve humanity. They provide us with guidance, or maps to follow, so that we may elevate our state of consciousness, in the hope that one day our state may be identical to theirs. Their goal for us is to live stress-free lives, bathed in light and love. The Great Beings have given endless talks and written countless books in the area of spirituality, so that we may come to know the way to experience daily life from our innermost nature, which is a state of incredible bliss and freedom. The words of the Great Beings are quite consistent from one time or one culture to another, which enhances our appreciation of the Truth resonating through their words.

Not all of us have direct access to the physical presence of a Great Being, but we can access their words, and incorporate them into our daily lives. We can imbibe these words as if they are speaking directly to us – they are! – and make it a practice to follow them. Following their words and teachings, we can take a journey on a spiritual path, a journey toward our inner Selves.

This book offers a series of 21 lessons, with each lesson being a steppingstone on a path to inner freedom; that is, freedom from stress and anxiety, as well as freedom from that which limits us in any way. These lessons are based on the words and teachings of Great Beings from various traditions, both from the East and the West. Thus, our intention is that, regardless of what religion one may practice, or whether one practices no formal religion, he or she can find meaning in the words of the wise ones throughout history. In this book, we examine the words from Christian, Hindu, Buddhist, and other traditions, which serve as anchors and guideposts in the experience of the Truth of Being.

Our primary purpose in this volume is to offer a spiritual approach to inner fulfillment as a series of steps or lessons, which range from those typically encountered by relative newcomers to a spiritual path to those encountered by seasoned practitioners of spirituality. The early lessons involve those that would confront almost anyone who questions what the purpose of a spiritual path is, and whether a "spiritual journey is for me." The lessons progress to cover topics most seekers discover, involving fears, worries, and questions as to whether they can succeed on a spiritual quest. The more advanced lessons involve the nature of the Inner Self, and the experience of unity of consciousness and peace. Finally, the most advanced lessons address issues of service to others and to oneself.

Although the lessons are presented in a sequence of ordered steps which appear to progress from early lessons to more advanced lessons, we do not claim that these lessons form an exclusive path toward spiritual unfoldment or enlightenment. In fact, many of those who profess to be 'enlightened' are quite specific in that there is no linear sequence, schedule, or road map to that state of awareness. We also recognize that there may be as many spiritual paths as there are seekers. The road to inner awakening—or enlightenment, or spiritual maturity—appears to be anything but a step-by-step process, as the lessons in this volume tend to suggest. Paradoxically, one might easily reverse the order of lessons in this book, and gain equally as much as one who follows the prescribed sequence.

These lessons were developed based on the experience of the writers: two clinical psychologists, each of whom has practiced a spiritual path in an Eastern tradition for more than 30 years. The authors have encountered the challenges contained in the lessons and have found that many spiritual practitioners eventually face most, or all, of the challenges on their spiritual journeys; thus, the lessons have great validity.

While reading a book on spirituality may be enjoyable, progress in spiritual development ultimately is based, to a great extent, on practices. Like any endeavor in life, one masters these lessons based on the time and effort one spends practicing them. Each lesson contains a group of activities or tasks; some are intended to be contemplated, and other tasks are intended to be more active and outer-directed. Please spend some time sitting with or being with the contemplation exercises. Close your eyes. See what thoughts, feelings, or bodily sensations arise as you contemplate. Give your soul an opportunity to assimilate and integrate the material in the contemplation exercises. So, please go 'beyond' a mere reading of the contemplations. Truly imbibe them as best you can.

How slowly or quickly one progresses in mastering the lessons depends on the individual. Some persons may choose to pursue a lesson per day, while other persons may spend a month on each lesson. Of course it is possible to complete all 21 lessons, and then start fresh with a 'beginner's mind' and re-engage with the teachings and the tasks in a deeper, more personal manner.

We know that from time immemorial, numerous teachers have recommended various steps their students can take on the path to God or 'enlightenment.' Some of these steps form the nucleus of these lessons and have been contemplated thoroughly by the authors, who are also spiritual students seeking enlightenment. It is our fervent hope that by reading the teachings, contemplating their meanings, and engaging with the tasks, you may progress toward a peaceful inner state.

The teachings presented in this book are those that have withstood the test of time. Each is a nugget of wisdom that we believe will speak to you, regardless of your situation in life. Whether you are an 'experienced seeker,' one who may have dabbled in a particular spiritual path, or a person trying to cope with stress or addiction, we hope this volume will speak to your needs. As psychologists, we looked for commonalities between spiritual lessons and current psychological theories and treatments. When possible, we highlighted the relationship between the spiritual and the psychological.

While we often speak of 'enlightenment,' 'awakening,' and Self-, or God-Realization,' we well understand that the attainment of the highest spiritual states is not to be found in reading a book or practicing various techniques. Moreover, we realize that the Great Beings make it clear that the highest states of consciousness cannot be described in words. Given these caveats, we recognize that increasing numbers of people now realize the significance of undertaking a spiritual journey is that it provides the best opportunity to understand the meaning of life, and overcome the psychological and other challenges life has to offer. We also recognize that countless people are opening to the materials presented in these chapters, which is evidenced by the proliferation of yoga studios and the increasing availability of meditation methods, such as Transcendental Meditation ™ and Mindfulness Based Stress Reduction (MBSR).

Much of the information presented in this volume is not found in articles in the popular press, and is intended for those persons who want to learn about their true identity. Thus some of the information will appear somewhat esoteric. We are guided in writing this book by the two words inscribed on the Temple of Apollo at Delphi in ancient Greece: "Know Thyself." In our opinions, there is no higher purpose in life and no calling that is more relevant from a psychological, sociological, or other purpose. More importantly, we regard human birth as very, very precious. Ancient scriptures regard a human birth as a rare gift to be nurtured and cherished. This point has been described by the contemporary Master teacher, Sai Maa:

> *A human life is precious. It is very important to understand that a human is to experience this life, this gift of life, this miracle of life, in a worthy way.*
>
> ***(Petals of Grace, p. 142)***

We intend that this volume will provide you with knowledge and tools to help you on a spiritual journey, whatever it is, and, in the process, will assist you in transcending many of life's everyday stressors.

Lesson One

MAKING FRIENDS WITH THE MIND

• • • • •

Illumination

The mind... "belongs to us, but is not who we really are. Just as a house belongs to us but is not us."

Dr. David Frawley

David Frawley, born in 1950, is a worldwide expert on Ayurveda, the Indian science of medicine. He has written over 30 books, and is the founder of the American Institute of Vedic studies in Santa Fe, New Mexico.

"There is no misery or suffering outside your own mind, because the whole world is nothing but a projection of your mind..."

Annamalai Swami

Annamalai Swami, 1906-1995, born in Tamil Nadu, India, ran away from home at age 17 to become a monk and was a direct disciple of Sri Ramana Maharshi. He realized the Self after many years of the practice of self-inquiry.

Examination

Understanding the nature of the mind poses, perhaps, the greatest conundrum, or greatest challenge, in human existence. Through the use of the mind, human beings appear to reach their pinnacle of success. Nobel prizes are won by creative people who have grasped new ideas and principles through the use of the mind. Innovations in science and technology are borne as gifts of persons' expert use of their minds. Incredible works in music and art seem to spring from the minds of exceptionally talented individuals. In all of existence, the human mind, typically considered the conscious mind in Western psychology, has emerged as the 'Sine qua non,' or the indispensable and ultimate step of human evolutionary development. Without any question, nothing in this world is as revered as "the human mind." Witness the explosion of popular books in neuroscience dedicated toward explaining the advances in our understanding of how the billions of neurons and trillions of synaptic connections in the brain operate together to allow the cortical and subcortical structures to function as one cohesive processor of information. All day long, we are dependent on our minds to complete mundane tasks, such as creating shopping lists, cooking meals, working at our jobs, and making plans for the future.

Perhaps the biggest fear many of us have is losing our mind, from events such as motor vehicle accidents to illnesses such as Alzheimer's disease or dementia. In Western society, one's greatest asset is having a good mind, and having a well-functioning mind is synonymous with good health.

There is probably no greater source of pain or confusion for a human being than trying to understand his or her mind. What is the mind after all? There is considerable controversy about this. There are some behavioral scientists who question whether the mind truly exists. They believe that the 'mind' is only an epiphenomenon associated with the brain. That is, some scientists believe that the emergence of human conscious awareness, reasoning, and thinking are fortunate accidental byproducts associated with the alignment of atoms, molecules, and other materials during the course of evolution.

The mind can be a person's greatest friend or greatest enemy.

Nevertheless, most of us intuitively know we possess a mind, even if it does not appear on an imaging study—such as an MRI. We know we have a mind because we refer to it all the time. We seek peace of mind. We change our minds. We feel that we may lose our mind! We pay someone no mind. In short, we take great pride in having a mind, and base our entire identity on the contents of our minds.

And what does the mind do? It thinks! Scientists estimate the mind produces thoughts, at the rate of 10,000 to 12,000 per day for the average person. We forget most of those thoughts, as they are inconsequential. However, many of those thoughts cause us a lot of problems, a lot of emotional pain. A highly-regarded and well-researched field of psychotherapy, known as cognitive therapy, has sprung up specifically to deal with troublesome irrational, dysfunctional thoughts, beliefs, and attitudes that cause or contribute to emotional pain and problems. Cognitive therapy has proven to be very effective for a wide range of human problems. We have shown that if we can change our thinking, then we can change our feelings and alter our mental and physical health. If we can learn to think positive, productive thoughts and eradicate negative, dysfunctional thoughts, we can become happier, experience a greater sense of well-being, and flourish—we can even become more spiritual. As the above quote indicates, as wonderful as the mind can be, it definitely has its limitations, and it can be dangerous. Thus, the mind can be a person's greatest friend or greatest enemy.

Dr. Frawley reassures us that we do not need to worry about how our minds disturb us. The reason is that, despite our insistence on identifying ourselves with the contents of our minds, and despite our insistence on whatever the mind happens to be thinking at the moment is both very important and true, the mind is not who we are! He says that who we truly are is something much different than can be imagined or idealized through the contents of our thoughts. In fact, because we are reminded by Great Beings, such as Annamalai Swami, that the mind, with its endless rumination and obsession over unpleasant subjects, is the cause of our suffering it is a tradition that the spiritual journey begins with a proper understanding of, and proper training to control, the mind.

Throughout history, learning to control the mind has been considered the most important attainment in the search for the Inner Self. Patanjali, a yoga master, wrote extensively about the mind in his book, 'The Yoga Philosophy of Patanjali.' In this work, compiled over 1500 years ago, Patanjali read all of the then-existing works on yoga and meditation, and distilled their essence, expressing the knowledge they contained in a concise series of aphorisms, or sutras. The first sutra explains that the purpose of yoga is to quiet the thoughts or fluctuations of the mind. Among all the varied topics described in Patanjali's sutras, none was of greater importance than learning to have a calm mind. He went on to say that when the mind is completely calm, the Inner Self, the experience of God, is spontaneously revealed. More importantly, it is this Inner Self, this Inner Divine Presence, that is our true nature; not the contents of our conscious mind.

All painful mental and emotional experience is self-created.

The Vedas, the ancient spiritual texts of India, provide us with two teachings regarding the nature of the mind that are nothing short of life-altering. Understanding these two teachings can utterly change your perception of life. The first, as Annamalai Swami also indicates, is that all of phenomenal reality can be construed as a projection of the mind. This is not to say that the world, and therefore our experience of it, is not real. It does indicate that everything we do experience is mediated through the mind—we never directly experience anything. Information we gather through our senses about the world around us falls upon the screen of our minds, and is then organized and understood uniquely by each individual. What we experience in our mind is a representation of reality, not reality itself. The representations we form about reality may be quite accurate or relatively inaccurate, but they are merely representations nevertheless. As Gregory Bateson, the esteemed anthropologist, reminded us, "The map is not the territory." Therefore, we cannot always take information our minds give us at face value: the information may be relatively correct or may be somewhat distorted.

Annamalai's quote suggests that our experiences of the outer world are all mediated through mental experience. The implication of this claim is that all painful mental and emotional experience is self-created; it is caused by the ways we interpret and ascribe meaning to personal and impersonal events. Thus, when we see negativity in the world, we are actually witnessing the negativity of our own thoughts and not necessarily the truth about what is truly occurring. In fact, Annamalai Swami regarded the mind as a shadow; again, as an entity that is not ultimately real. Therefore, he recommended the avoidance of attempts to catch and control the mind, as they would be exercises in futility.

The second life-transforming fact regarding the human mind is that it is NOT the highest level of evolutionary development that humans are capable of attaining. According to the Vedas, the classical Indian (Hindu) spiritual texts there are six levels of subjectivity in life. They are as follows:

- The Senses.
- Emotions.
- Intellect.
- Mind.
- Ego.
- Higher Self.

We incorporate information into the body through the five senses, what we can see, hear, feel, taste, and touch. Our feelings or emotions are subtler than the senses, and in many ways they are an extension of them, combined with thoughts and other psychological experiences. The intellect entails the use of discrimination and discernment. We collectively experience all of the information developed from our senses, feelings, and intellect through the process of what we call the mind. The possessor of the mind is the self (the small self) or ego. The ego is our definition of who we are. For example, in common parlance, we might say, "I have made up my mind." The self or ego is the one who experiences the mind.

The subtlest level of existence is what is known as the Self (with a capital S), or sometimes, Higher Self. This is roughly equivalent to what we know as a soul in the West. The Self is pure Consciousness, pure Awareness. It is unbounded. Its nature is pure bliss. Realizing that our true identity is the Higher Self is the goal of all spiritual pursuits. The nature of the Self is described in Hindu philosophy as **Satchitananda: existence, consciousness, and bliss.**

According to an ancient philosophical system, the human mind is not the highest level of creation.

In a somewhat different, but related, philosophical system from ancient India, Kashmir Shaivism, all of creation can be conceptualized into a series of 34 levels (tattvas) arranged in a sort of hierarchical order from the highest or most subtle levels to the lowest or most gross levels. The levels reveal the unfolding or involution of Supreme Consciousness throughout creation. When I first learned about the tattvas, I was surprised to learn that in this system, the human intellect is not the highest level. At the highest level, the Shiva tattva, is Pure Consciousness in which there is no difference between a subject (the knower) or an object (the known). This is the level of satchitananda. God rests at peace with His/Her own Being, so to speak. At the lowest levels of creation are the five gross elements: air, earth, water, fire, and ether. The mind, intellect, and the ego are at levels 14-16 in this classificatory system. These level include many of the processes – sensation, perception, attention, discrimination, logic, etc. – that are studied by Western cognitive scientists and neuroscientists. The point of knowing this information is that there are many higher levels of knowledge and spiritual attainment available to human beings that are well beyond the capability of the conscious mind. We are not finished products by any stretch of the imagination. We can go higher!

We know ourselves, others, and the world around us in terms of the mind. All reality is structured by the mind, shaped by it. Thus the mind is a tool, a means of organizing our day-to-day experience, just as a hammer and a saw help us to build and repair physical objects. According to the great psychologist William James, the world is experienced by an infant as a "blooming, buzzing confusion," until the mind sorts it out and organizes it as the infant develops. The mind is not a passive process—it is quite active. However, its processes are all affected by environmental **conditioning.** Our ways of experiencing ourselves and others are habits that have been conditioned or trained over periods of many years. While some of these habits are beneficial and productive, others are not. For instance, having been conditioned to see ourselves as failures if we do not succeed on a task is unlikely to be beneficial, but having learned we can succeed if we 'try, try again' likely is.

The realm of the Inner Self (at the highest tattva) lies beyond any and all human mental conditioning and beyond the mind itself. Through spiritual practices, such as meditation and contemplation, we learn to **transcend the conditioning** of the mind, to go beyond an understanding of ourselves and the environment based upon what we have learned. This is a profound and provocative statement! We learn to purify the mind so that it will reflect Pure Consciousness, which underlies the mind and gives it its reality, much as the sun warms, energizes, and makes the very earth possible.

Most people's minds are continually engaged in thinking, or are agitated and anxious. A stirred-up mind distorts our perception of reality. The way to peace and serenity, therefore, is to calm or still the mind. An excellent analogy here is that of a pool of water. When you gaze into a completely calm, still pond, you can see the very bottom of it. However, if you drop a stone in the pond, that clarity is immediately disturbed. Some of the mud at the bottom of the pond may be stirred up, further clouding the clarity of the water. In the same way, when we engage in spiritual practices, we bring clarity, stillness, and purity to our minds, and they become, or can become, perfect reflectors of Pure Consciousness.

The first step on the spiritual journey is learning about the nature of the mind, and taking steps to extricate ourselves from its conditioned patterns. We learn that we cannot 'think our way' into an awakened or advanced spiritual state. We also learn that there is so much more to us, to our existence, than our capacity to think or what the mind tells us about who we really are. As we engage in practices to bring the mind under greater control, our mental and physical health improves substantially, and we experience deeper levels of our own existence, well beyond the level of conscious thought.

Contemplation

1. Think of a time when you had the experience of a peaceful mind. How did this happen? Were you in a peaceful setting, such as a park or a beach? What was the experience like? Did you have peaceful thoughts -- or no thoughts at all? Were you aware of your mind?
2. Chuang Tse has said, "To the mind that is still, the whole universe surrenders..." How do your perceptions and experiences change when your mind is quieted?

Application

1. Sit comfortably in a chair or cross-legged on the floor. Relax and breathe gently for about five minutes. Now say the word "I." Now just think it. Allow your attention to focus on the word "I." Just observe what you think; watch your thoughts. Let them come and go. Simply note them. Now become aware of what you feel and what you see around you: what you smell, hear, touch, taste; but just note the sensations -- be uninvolved with them, as if these things were happening to someone else -- much as if you are listening to someone else's conversation in the next room, uninvolved with it. Don't get involved with your own mind. Just notice what transpires during this practice for about 15 minutes. Just simply be with this awareness. Please have no expectations for what might happen, or what might not happen.
2. For ten minutes, observe your thoughts. Watch how they evolve, fluctuate, move, and change. Take a 'witnessing,' not a 'judgmental,' attitude. Avoid the notion that some thoughts are better than others. See each of your thoughts as the same,

as distracting conditions which interfere with seeing who you truly are.

3. Observe what happens to your mind during different types of activity, such as exercise, knitting, reading, conversation, and something as simple as walking -- just be aware of the processes of your mind.
4. Based on your above experiences: how would you describe your own mind? Is it one of frequent contentment, or do thoughts of worry and despair predominate? What types of thoughts do you have about yourself? Are they uplifting, or do they tend to be self-deprecating?

Lesson Two

LEARNING TO SURRENDER

• • • • •

Illumination

"To hold, you must first open your hand. Let go."

Lao Tzu

Lao Tzu was an ancient Chinese philosopher who lived around the 6th century BC. He is the reputed author of the Tao Te Ching or Book of Proverbs, and the founder of the philosophy of Taoism.

"It is the very attempt to have power which makes us powerless. And it is the abandonment of all attempts to have power which blends us with the cosmic power: which conquers all..."

Vernon Howard

Vernon Howard, 1918-1992, was an American author and philosopher from the 20th century. He emphasized the release of the "false self" and "conditioned ego" as a means to move into a higher spiritual life, or a 'New Life.'

"The greatness of a man's power is the measure of his surrender."

William Booth

William Booth, 1829-1912, was an 18th century British Methodist preacher who founded the Salvation Army and became its first General.

Examination

After the mind starts to come under greater control, we may start to experience a measure of contentment, and start to believe that there truly is more to our existence than we experience at the level of conscious thought. But, as we noted in Chapter 1, we cannot think our way into a more advanced spiritual state. At some point, it starts to become evident that we need help from someone or something else—a Master teacher, Enlightened Guru, or from God or Source* itself. This is the start of the process of surrender: the realization that we need help, and are willing to open up to it.

For some, when it comes to embarking on a spiritual journey, the word 'Surrender' is often an immediate showstopper. Here in the West, where we have been trained to be independent, think for ourselves, and develop our autonomy and leadership skills, the word 'surrender' is taboo and to be avoided at all costs. For many people, the word surrender conjures images of quitting, giving up, failing, and losing. Surrender is for vanquished people and weaklings—the losers of fights and battles, as we have learned throughout history. Recalling images of surrender, such as the painting in the US Capitol of British General Cornwallis surrendering to the American patriots at Yorktown, Virginia, ending the American Revolutionary War, is a vivid reminder of how devastating the process of surrender can be. Because we have been trained to associate the word surrender with defeat, we believe that when we surrender, we have lost to another person, group, or country. Surrender means we have been defeated by 'another.' No wonder any of us would turn away when we hear this word.

> Surrender…indicates the start of an exciting transformative process.

A number of persons attempting 12-step programs have difficulty with Step 2 ('Surrender to a higher power') simply because of the word surrender, regardless of their beliefs about the existence of a Higher Power. Interestingly, we have worked with many people, including members of the clergy, who would not even dream of attempting a spiritual program that incorporates the word 'surrender.'

On the spiritual journey, the word surrender has an entirely different meaning. Whereas in everyday life the word surrender typically invokes images of submission to a vanquishing conqueror, on the spiritual path the word surrender means just the opposite. Surrender on the spiritual quest indicates a new beginning, openness, and the start of an exciting, transformative process. The process involves the beginnings of a shift in identity, from the small self to the Great Self.

Over the course of our lives, all of us have developed self-concepts, which entail negative or limiting features. We have learned these concepts consciously and unconsciously, from often well-intentioned family members, teachers, friends, and others. Who has not thought of themselves, at least from time to time, as inferior, weak, incapable, and helpless? We sometimes believe, incorrectly, that in identifying with these limited concepts we are practicing true 'humility' and exemplifying a genuine religious or spiritual attitude, as if the more we 'put ourselves down,' the humbler and more spiritually advanced we are. In actuality, these patterns of thought have nothing to do with humility, religion, or spirituality. They simply serve to allow the limited 'ego' to believe it is in control and 'on the job.' We essentially believe in a story about who we are, which is often a negative story, and believe it is fantasy to think we are anything other than someone who is basically ineffective. These thoughts are consistent with negative mood states and depression. The fact is that the more we focus and concentrate on negative thoughts, the more depressed we become. Why do we think it is wrong to question the negative stories as to who we truly are?

Through the process of 'letting go,' as Lao Tzu suggests, we release or eliminate that within us that is false or untrue. Invariably, that which is untrue binds us to living life in a restricted manner. The greatest 'untruths' about ourselves involve limiting labels ('stupid,' 'crazy,' 'failure,' 'incompetent,' etc.). For instance, believing ourselves to be 'addicts' who are dependent upon a drug for our happiness is considered untrue, as it is inconsistent with our highest nature. Furthermore, viewing ourselves as angry and mean-spirited is considered untrue, as it is inconsistent with our genuine nature of being pure love. Quite often, when we embrace a limiting conception of ourselves, we attempt, in an unconscious manner, to live up to that limited conception. For example, most of us have known at one time or another an individual who considered himself 'stupid,' and seemingly acted in a ridiculous manner simply to live up to that verbal label.

On the spiritual journey, one of the key aspects of surrender entails giving up self-concepts involving limitation and weakness. The truth of the matter is that these concepts are acquired in life through the processes of learning and social conditioning, but they are completely inconsistent with our true identity and the goal of spiritual practice.

The meditation Master, Swami Muktananda, entitled one of his books, *'Getting Rid of What You Haven't Got.'* This title appears to epitomize one of the essential spiritual tasks: the elimination, or surrender, of what we do not own or is not an intrinsic part of our true Self—ideas about limitation, lack, inferiority, and all negative characteristics we might use in defining ourselves. In this book, Muktananda writes about what is attained on the spiritual search. He says, "The truth is that we get what we have already got, not what we haven't got (p. 10)." It appears to be somewhat of a paradox that we 'get' what we already have, what our true nature eternally is: a being imbued with truth, love, and bliss. In contrast, we do not get any more of what is not inimical to our true nature: ideas about our shortcomings, inabilities, and weaknesses.

When our surrender of egoic concepts involving limitation is complete, the door is opened to identification with our inner Divinity. Using his complete identification with his own inner greatness, Lord Jesus was able to proclaim, "I and the Father are One."

> When we let go of our need to control power, we are like a river flowing into the ocean.

That surrender actually opens the door to the acquisition of power appears counterintuitive; this is because the concept of power is very much misunderstood. Today, there is much talk of empowering people, or helping them to feel capable of pursuing their hopes and dreams. On the spiritual quest, it is important to understand that power is not necessarily control. Exerting power is not a means to make others submit to our will; nor is it a means to acquire all of our hearts' desires. In a way, recognizing our powerlessness can be a strength, not a weakness. For example, trying to control the uncontrollable, such as an addictive disease or other people, is folly. Trying to make our children live the lives we want them to live can be an exercise in great frustration. We are not the generators of power, much as we may like to think we are. As Jesus of Nazareth remarked to Pontius Pilate, you have no power of your own—any power you have comes to you from far beyond.

Power exists, to be sure. But when it comes to spiritual matters, we must give up the need to generate personal power and control. Wielding power suggests that we have something to protect, to guard, to possess. It is time to let go of the need for power; or, more correctly, the illusion of power. Jesus said, "Whosoever shall lose his life shall find it..." The simple truth is that we are limited in our ability to accomplish much in life completely of our own accord. We do not even possess the power to keep ourselves alive. When we let go of our need to wield power, we are like a river flowing into the ocean. We let go. We go with the flow. We surrender to the Truth or the will of God. We enjoy the ride and eventually enjoy the Power or energy that exists beyond our ego, and self-control that activates our life and, indeed, all of life.

When we attempt to control our lives, we are alone. We are unsupported by nature. When we let go, when we "let go and let God," so to speak, we begin to move in the direction of spiritual union. We relinquish our attachment to personal power. This may sound counterintuitive—after all, everyone wants to feel a sense of power, to have power in their lives. But ego-driven power comes at a high price, and it's too high of a price to pay. As the great saint Shantidasa said, "Surrendering yourself to God is giving up what you can't keep for what you can't lose." Our true energy and power comes from surrender/attunement/alignment to a Higher Power, and through that process, our hearts and minds expand. In contrast, a closed heart and mind trap energy, and render it immobile. True power, therefore, is powerlessness—we give up the need for self-willed power. As Satchidananda said, "The moment you stop wanting anything, you have your Self!"

The reason any spiritual practice, such as meditation, prayer, or contemplation works is that we let go of personal control. We let go of possessing power. We realize that our ego and our mind are powerless to accomplish the greatest tasks in life, the attunement and merging with our true inner nature. We stop fighting, we stop resisting, and we transcend or go beyond our limited self-will. We back off and let the divine power that runs the universe take over. This is true surrender; this is the real meaning of powerlessness. Let's face it. We have no power or control over most things in life. Have you ever tried to control your mind, even for a few seconds? Have you ever tried to control another person to make them feel or think a certain way, to change their behavior, to conform to your demands? It simply does not and cannot work. On the other hand, we do have **influence and free will.**

However, influence is quite different from power and control. For example, if we have a medical condition, such as diabetes, we are not able to control it, but we can influence its expression by engaging in behaviors that will keep it stable, such as taking insulin regularly and eating the right kinds of foods on schedule. The body can heal, then, through the power of God.

With regard to spirituality, we cannot directly command our minds, our bodies, and our spirits to become instantaneously free and enlightened. But we can influence all of these factors through the disciplined pursuit of spiritual practices. We can make the process of surrender a daily practice, and in this way open up to the Truth a little more each day. The important aspect is that we **actively** surrender to the truth. As Sri Aurobindo, the 20th century Indian saint, suggests in his book *'The Mother,'* surrender is not a matter of waiting for God to do the surrendering for us. In fact, he emphasizes that "...out of an inert passivity nothing true and powerful can come." Over time, we learn to surrender one part of ourselves, then another part, then another, etc., until one day we awaken to the fact that we have surrendered ourselves to the will of God in totality.

> No one goes it alone in life. We all need a Higher Power.

We are often taught and conditioned to rely on our own personal willpower and resources to get our needs met in life.

Self-reliance and independence are highly prized in our culture. Consider the adage: "If you want something done right, do it yourself!" However, when we carefully examine this notion, we find it to be an illusion. No one goes it alone in life. No one gets very far in any endeavor without giving up the idea of complete self-control and enlisting the help of others. Therefore, give up the pursuit of being completely self-reliant. Get beyond the illusion of independence. We all need one another. We all need a higher power. We all need contact with our Source, where all power originates. And, paradoxically, the path to accessing the power of Source comes through surrender; it comes through acceptance of powerlessness. This is an extremely profound, but mostly misunderstood, spiritual concept. When we become completely surrendered or aligned with the power of Source, we then gain access to true power.

In 1983, I (Vincent) met my spiritual teacher face-to-face for the first time. In that moment, I experienced surrender. It was completely unexpected. I knew without a doubt that I would want to be her student, and study spiritual teachings with her. Surrender has helped me to understand that I am not alone on my spiritual journey, and that while I must do the work, my teacher is always with me, encouraging and supporting me. Through surrender, then, I have learned little by little to release the false idea of being all alone, and embrace the idea that I am connected to and a part of a greater whole.

*Throughout this book, reference to Supreme Consciousness will be made by using various synonyms, such as 'God,' 'Source,' 'Higher Self,' etc.

Contemplation

1. Spend some time thinking about the health problems we confront in life: for example, cancer, heart disease, and addiction. It is important to realize that we cannot directly fight these disorders. We cannot directly control them or eradicate them, but we can influence them. We can go over them, around them, under them -- ultimately we have to transcend them. It would be madness to step into a boxing ring with the heavyweight champion and try to battle it out with him -- he would knock our block off! We would have to come up with an alternate plan. We would have to focus on what we can do—perhaps find his weakness, find his psychological fears and use them against him—or even run for our lives! It's really no good pretending that we have power when we really don't.
2. Think about this: can you stop time? Can you keep yourself alive forever? Can you control someone's mind? Can you stop your own heart? Can you stop the earth from spinning on its axis? Of course not. You can do none of these things. Try to control your own thoughts, your own mind, sometime. Better yet, try to control someone else's thoughts and mind -- it simply does not work. We should take the advice of Lao Tzu – "flow around obstacles, don't confront them."
3. Try this exercise: close your eyes and be silent for a few minutes. Think of a problem in your life that you initially fought against and resisted but eventually accepted. How did it feel, fighting it? How did it feel when you let go? What ultimately happened? We save energy and we are happier when we give up useless struggles. This is true for life in

general as well. As the great mythologist Joseph Campbell said, "We must give up the life we planned to have the life that awaits us."

4. Spend some time thinking about your upbringing. How were you conditioned and what were you taught, with regard to fighting problems in life? Were you taught that a truly strong person does not need or accept assistance from anyone? How does that conditioning affect how you tackle problems today?
5. What are you afraid will happen if you really surrender? That is, what are you afraid will happen if you really accept a particular problem and stop resisting it, or trying to control it? Your answer to this question will tell you a lot about yourself.

Application

1. Meditation on the breath --

   Take a few minutes and notice your breathing. Notice how effortless it is. You do not have to try to breathe -- you do not have to control it. It simply happens, all on its own. It comes, it goes. You breathe in, you breathe out—there is no volition. Your lungs expand—your lungs contract. Our breathing is much like the ocean; constantly washing the shore, pausing momentarily, and then ceaselessly flowing back upon itself, to no end.

   Spend the next 15 minutes just innocently, effortlessly observing your breathing. Just be mindful of it. Notice it. Observe it. This is called 'breathing with awareness,' or 'conscious breathing.' It may be the single most important spiritual exercise you ever undertake, in terms of the reward accruing to your body and mind. If you begin getting lost in thought, simply come back to this gentle awareness of the constant flowing in and flowing out of your breath.

As you watch your breath, you may find your abdomen is spontaneously moving up and down in tandem with the breath. At this point, you are engaged in what is called diaphragmatic breathing, or "belly breathing." This is the more effortless, natural way to breathe. It is the way newborn babies breathe. If you do not spontaneously begin to breathe in this manner, pay extra attention to both your chest and your abdomen area. Notice which area moves as you breathe. You can place your hand (or a book if you are lying down) on your abdomen as you breathe and see if your abdomen rises or inflates as you inhale. Give yourself a lot of time to gently watch how you are breathing. To make the shift to diaphragmatic breathing, it is more important to 'surrender' by noticing and watching how you are breathing than to force or coax any sudden change. An ability to accept how you are breathing in any given moment opens the door for your body to naturally shift and change of its own accord.

2. Today find someone in your life with whom you have been fighting or resisting. Deliberately find a way to accept him/her without trying to change that person. Stop fighting this individual, although you may disagree with his/her position. Recognize the validity of the other's position, without judging the person as wrong, stupid, inferior, or bad. This work may be completed on an internal basis or on an external one. Remember that one skilled in debate can take any position to support or defend without becoming personally involved. As you move into acceptance of the other person, spend some time noticing how you feel. Do you feel freer or lighter?

3. Go through your house or garage or office and deliberately discard or give away something that you have been meaning to get rid of for some time. Notice how you feel when you do this.
4. Today spend two hours doing whatever comes to your mind without any plans, goals, strategies, or directions.
5. Identify three limiting beliefs you hold about yourself. Typically, the beliefs begin with the words "I cannot..." or "I am... (lowly, weak, inferior, etc.)" Spend two minutes engaging in the following exercise. Mentally repeat the limiting thought, and then surrender the thought by gently informing yourself that the thought is an illusion. Now think of the opposite belief – e.g., "I am strong" is the opposite of "I am weak"—and recall a time you felt strong. Meditate on your own feeling of strength as felt in this memory.
6. Sit for two to three minutes and reflect on one or more times in which you received unexpected help in your life from someone else. The help may have come in a very small way; perhaps it was something as trivial as a person holding a door open for you when you were carrying a heavy bundle. Make it a regular practice to contemplate the various times you have received unsolicited outside assistance. Notice how your attitude toward life changes as you engage in this practice.
7. Close your eyes, take a few conscious breaths, and slowly repeat the following phrase: "I am in God (you may substitute any word here to stand for Supreme Consciousness), and God is in me." Repeat several times. Allow the vibration of this statement to permeate your entire being for several minutes, and notice how you feel. Next, take a few breaths, and slowly

repeat the following phrase three times: "I AM." Again, let these vibrations permeate your entire being and notice how you feel.

Lesson Three

DEALING WITH FEAR

• • • • •

Illumination

"What do you have to fear? Nothing. Whom do you have to fear? No one. Why? Because whosoever has joined forces with God obtains three great privileges: omnipotence without power, intoxication without lying, and life without death ..."

St. Francis of Assisi

Born in Italy and regarded as one of the greatest Catholic Saints, Francis, 1181-1226, was a friar and a preacher. He founded several religious orders, including the Franciscan Order. He is associated with the patronage of animals and the environment, and he is the patron saint of Italy.

Examination

In his inaugural address in 1933, in the midst of the Great Depression, President Franklin Roosevelt proclaimed, "...

the only thing we have to fear is... fear itself." At a time when there was plenty to fear, both internally – joblessness, poverty, homelessness – as well as externally – global depression, nationalist movements in Europe – President Roosevelt essentially told the American people that we could overcome our problems by working our way out of them. Contrast that approach with the rhetoric our candidates from both parties are using on the campaign trail in 2016. Candidates are discussing building walls, taking back jobs from other countries, and making America great again (implying that we are no longer great). No matter which candidate one might support, it is clear that the populace is being told there is a lot to fear. Therefore, if you are one of many people who are fearful and anxious, there are likely many good reasons for feeling the way you do. Today, most patients who come to our offices complain of anxiety and fear. This was not the case twenty or more years ago.

One of the many reasons for starting on a spiritual path is to overcome fear (of anything and everything). If you believe that fear is a natural part of life, is unavoidable, and to be expected, most people would agree with you. But you would be flat wrong! The reason you would be wrong isn't because there are challenging circumstances out there with which we must deal, but because despite the outer circumstances, fear is internally generated; and in that regard, we have a lot of choice.

Throughout the ages, great beings and sages from all the world religions and traditions have given us a similar message about fear: fear simply doesn't exist. In our modern age, this assertion seems completely preposterous. How many persons do you know who would profess to have no fear? Certainly the fact that the mood tranquilizer, Abilify, is the top-selling prescription drug is a testament to the fact that many, many people find anxiety and mood problems, which certainly contain elements of fear, to be quite real. There are websites which contain large lists of all known phobias (fears). There are names for fears of gravity (barophobia), clowns (coulrophobia), and teenagers (ephebiphobia). The latter phobia is hopefully amenable to treatment.

> Many of our fears are learned over time through a process of conditioning.

Many psychologists have long considered fear as, by and large, a conditioned, or learned response to a situation. In 1920, psychologists John Watson and Rosalie Rayner taught a nine-month-old child, Albert, to become fearful of a white rat in a brief amount of time. Initially, Albert enjoyed playing with the rat. Subsequently, whenever Albert touched the rat, the experimenters made a loud sound behind his back. Albert responded to the noise by crying and showing fear. After repeatedly pairing the two stimuli – the rat and the loud sound – Albert began showing a fear response as soon as the rat entered the room (that is, Albert began to anticipate the noxious loud sound). Many days later, Albert also showed a fear response when presented with other objects – a rabbit, a coat, a seal-skinned coat, and even the experimenter in a Santa Claus hat – which resembled the rat in some way. This experiment was perhaps the first to demonstrate that fear can be conditioned in humans, and that a fear response can generalize from the original feared object to other objects that resemble the feared object in some manner. No doubt human beings have fears that are unconditioned – the loud noise in the experiment with little Albert, wild animals, violence, etc. However, experiments such as Watson and Rayner's demonstrated that perhaps many of our fears are learned over time, through a process of conditioning.

Many of our contemporary fears involve social anxiety: a fear of being in the presence of others, especially those we don't know very well. Many of us fear being judged negatively. We worry others won't approve of us or like us, and we often cope by avoiding social situations. Sometimes, when we cannot avoid social situations, we self-medicate with alcohol and drugs; indeed, many alcoholics discover newfound confidence in the presence of strangers while under the influence. Alcohol inhibits our fearful reactions around others; and it is no surprise that there are people who become addicted to alcohol because it helps them cope with unfamiliar people at work and in social settings. In fact, some alcoholics who would otherwise be shy around others are suddenly the life of the party. No wonder alcohol is so reinforcing.

Perhaps as important as the fact that fear can be conditioned is the fact that fear can become unconditioned, or unlearned. Psychologists often refer to the eradication of a learned response as extinction. In the case of little Albert, his fear response could have been extinguished by exposing him to the rat repeatedly, without the accompanying loud noise. Sooner or later, Albert likely would have abandoned his fear reactions, as they were no longer reinforced. The process of extinction is involved in the procedure with which many psychologists currently treat fears and phobias: Exposure Therapy. This therapy, in brief, requires the patient to spend time in the presence of the feared stimulus, while tolerating the unpleasant feelings of fear. After repeated exposures to the feared stimulus, the fearful reactions extinguish, and the fear essentially dissolves.

Except for some of our primal reactions, most of our worries, anxieties, phobias, and fears are learned. But surely you have noticed that each of us differs in terms of what we might fear. Some of us are afraid of heights; some are afraid of public speaking; some are afraid of flying; some are afraid of bridges; small spaces; the dark; and the list goes on. But there are those who do not fear heights or public speaking or flying. Is this not evidence that fear does not need to be a permanent aspect of our existence?

Many of us are aware that throughout history there have been Great Beings, such as St. Francis, who have lived on this earth without fear. For the most part, we relegate these Great Beings to the dust bowl of history, as if it would be impossible now for anyone to live a life without fear. Once again, this would be an incorrect conclusion. There are increasing numbers of people living on this planet today in an awakened or enlightened state who live without fear, and are eager to let us know that we can live the same way.

In her recent book *When Fear Falls Away*, Jan Frazier speaks about an awakening, which occurred after she had intense worries about the possibility of a cancer diagnosis. In the Introduction she writes about feeling tormented on the inside, worrying about her children's welfare, her health, and money. She dreaded both her own death and the deaths of those she loved. Following her awakening, she lost all of her fears and experienced intense joy while engaged in the simplest tasks of everyday life. She described enlightenment as a state of unwavering wellbeing that carries on, independent of whatever is going on in the realm of familiar life.

Vidya Frazier, in her book *The Art of Letting Go: A Pathway to Inner Freedom,* describes experiencing intense suffering, doubt, and emotional reactivity for years prior to 'awakening.' She notes that "most of my response to life prior to awakening were based on fear—fear of people, things, situations, poverty, violence. Now all that is gone. It was replaced by a miraculous sense of trust in life itself, a knowing that I would be okay no matter what might happen to my body or my life" (p. 14).

While it is true that, in both cases, these individuals engaged in spiritual practices, it also is true that they were 'ordinary people' with 'ordinary problems,' just like you and me. Neuroscience researcher Jill Bolte Taylor, in her TED talk, reported experiencing a changed life, following a stroke in which she experienced massage damage in the left hemisphere of her brain. Forced to experience existence through her intact right hemisphere, she experienced reality as a totality of bliss, unity, and beauty, which was devoid of all fear.

While we could easily find similar experiences and quotes from other awakened/enlightened people to discuss, the point is that it seems more and more people are awakening on this planet. Moreover, there are many people who are perhaps not in an enlightened state, but who, nevertheless, have found that fear has all but exited from their experience of life.

The science of yoga says that fear is a distortion in our thinking and perception. In other words, fear is rooted in ignorance. There is a classic tale in India, which is really an analogy, known as the story of the snake in the rope. One day, a monk was meditating in his cave, in the faint light of the dawn. He peered into the corner of the cave and spied something coiled up, resting on the floor.

He thought to himself in an alarmed manner, "It's a snake, it's a snake!" Although he was immediately frightened, he managed to compose himself, lit a candle, and took a second look at the coiled object in the corner of the cave: it was only a piece of coiled up rope! In a split second, his alarm and fear dissipated as his intellect and perception gained clarity. He experienced a mistake of the intellect. He had succumbed to the distortions in his mind. In the Sanskrit language of the Vedas, the ancient Indian scriptures, fear is considered a mistake of the intellect --pragyaparag. Fear is one of the many mental and physiological imbalances that blocks our recognition of who we truly are at the root of our being. This recognition is labeled Self-Realization. There have been those among us – saints, sages, and ordinary persons – who live in a permanent state of Self-Realization.

Yoga says the antidote to fear is to still or calm the many waves of thoughts that continually wash over the mind. When the mind is still, we slip effortlessly past fear and we begin to merge with our innermost Self or God. In Patanjali's book on the yoga sutras, recall that the first sutra explained that the purpose of meditation is to quiet all the thought waves or thought vibrations in the mind. The second yoga sutra goes on to say that when the mind is completely still, the Seer abides in Itself, or rests in its own True Nature. That is, our true nature is automatically seen or revealed in the absence of thought patterns.

In the state of the Inner Self, we have no fear. We experience intoxication, omnipotence, and immortality, as St. Francis noted. As Jill Bolte Taylor described, we experience ourselves not as individuals, but as "all that is, the life force power of the universe." How often have you seen statues of the smiling Buddha in Asian (mostly Chinese) restaurants? He has that big belly, and he looks so happy. We think he is happy because he has eaten so much delicious food. While perhaps we, too, might be happy if we consumed a large quantity of delicious food, that is not why the Budda is smiling. The Buddha is in a state of bliss because he has gained complete mastery over the mind, and rendered it as calm as the calmest sea. He is an example of what we, too, might accomplish, with complete mastery of our minds.

For those of you who wish to start to reduce the amount of fear in your life, the meditation on the breath exercise presented in the last chapter is an excellent starting point. If that exercise can become a part of your daily routine, you will likely notice a difference in your response to life within a few weeks or months. Breathing meditations have recently been found to help even those individuals coping with severe amounts of fear, such as is found in Posttraumatic Stress Disorder (PTSD). Dr. Emma Seppalla and her colleagues, as published in the Journal of Traumatic Stress, examined 21 American veterans from the wars in Iraq and Afghanistan as they participated in a breathing-based meditation. The 21 participants met for three-hour sessions over seven days. Researchers measured eye-blink responses to loud noises, respiration rates, and self-reported descriptions of participants' PTSD symptoms. Assessments were taken at four intervals – before, during, one month later, and one year after the treatment. The breathing meditation resulted in reduced PTSD symptoms of anxiety, and respiration rate showed the strongest effect on hyperarousal and the recurrence of traumatic memories and nightmares. These findings are extremely valuable as individuals returning from wartime conditions with PTSD suffer from many symptoms, and psychiatric medications are of limited effectiveness with this population.

Contemplation

1. Julius Caesar said it is better to suffer the worst of a situation all at once than to live in perpetual fear of it. What has been your experience of avoiding fear? Does it grow? Are you trapped by it?
2. Everyone at some time or another is afraid, but some do not let it stop them. Jesus of Nazareth said, "Do not be afraid for I am with you, every day, even until the end of time." He understood fear, for he himself was afraid when he contemplated his own death through crucifixion. Yet he faced his fear, transcended it, and triumphed over it! He set the example for us.
3. Ralph Waldo Emerson said—do the thing you fear... and the death of fear is certain... Again, we are encouraged to face our fears squarely, to challenge them, and to see them for what they are rather than to allow them to rule our lives. And through this confrontation, we get a bit closer to freedom. When you confronted a fear in the past, what happened? Was it as bad as you thought? What did you learn and how did you change to resolve that experience? Have you ever tried to make yourself deliberately engage in an activity you found frightening (rock climbing, windsurfing, etc.)? What was your experience when you completed the activity?
4. What is it that causes fear to go away? Whether we overcome a feared object/experience through Exposure Therapy, re-experiencing it, or viewing it through candlelight, there is something inside each of us that causes fear to go away. Some call this the Light of Conscious Awareness. What name would you ascribe to it?

5. All fears are based upon personal experiences that have occurred in the past. If all of our awareness is completely consumed in the present moment, there is almost no room for fear.

Application

1. Over the next 24 hours do one thing that elicits mild to moderate fear in you. Make sure you select something that will not be harmful to you or others. What happened? How did your feelings and behavior change?
2. Write down your own definition of fear. Imagine a Martian is visiting the earth, and he has no idea what fear is! How would you define and describe it to him?
3. List your top five fears -- now rank them from highest to lowest. Beside each fear write down how you would feel if that particular fear actualized. What would be the worst case scenario with each fear? What are the possibilities and probabilities of this fear becoming a reality? Beside each fear, write down what plans you would have to deal with it if it became a reality. Note how you feel and any changes in your thinking after you complete this exercise.
4. Think of a fearful situation. Feel the fear... intensify it, allow it to amplify... now fade it away until it is barely noticeable... and begin to replace it, to supplant it with love... allow the feeling of love to grow, to become more acute, become stronger. Note any changes in your feeling and thinking. Patanjali, the author of the Yoga sutras, advises us, when confronted with a fearful or other negative situation, to simply lean in the other direction. Once we have done this, allow your mind to take on a quality opposite to the negative one.

5. Choose one of your greatest fears. Imagine yourself sitting in a large movie theatre by yourself, and the thing that you fear is up on the screen, larger-than-life, in living color! Make it extremely large and extremely colorful, exaggerate it. Now take your fear and transform it from living color to black and white. Start to see the image fade. See it fade a bit more until it's barely noticeable; you can barely make it out. Now... very quickly flash the screen to a huge picture of 'You.' Quickly switch it back to living color, make it as large as you can, see yourself with wonderful qualities. You are happy, strong, alert, growing bigger and bigger and bigger! You are in bold, living color, filling the screen, spilling over the screen, and filling up the entire earth! Do this several times with several of your greatest fears. After you're finished, go back to your fears and notice if anything has changed -- do you feel less afraid? Do you feel any less threatened? Does the grip of the fear seem less tight?
6. Think of one of your fears. Perhaps you might begin with one of your smaller ones. Allow yourself to tolerate the discomfort or anxiety that accompanies the thought for as long as you can. Notice what is happening as you tolerate the feeling. Tolerate this feeling until it suddenly disappears. You may have to repeat this exercise in small doses. Even a few moments of tolerating a fear will reduce its hold over you.
7. Engage in the Meditation on the Breath exercise from Chapter 2. Notice as you do this if any fears come to mind. When they arise, do not chase them away. Simply allow them to be in your conscious awareness and gently move your awareness back to the breath. Experience yourself breathing in and breathing out.

Lesson Four

ON SUFFERING

• • • • •

Illumination

"Suffering gives us the impetus to escape from our self-limiting ignorance. If God did not send these gifts of suffering and misery, many people would be content to live their whole lives alienated from God and ignorant of their true nature..."

Annamalai Swami

Examination

Nobody wants to experience pain and suffering. Trying to perceive suffering as 'gifts' from God can be a true stretch of the imagination. Most of us sincerely question how a benevolent God permits so much suffering, so many tragedies, and so much cruelty in this world.

> There must be some purpose, some reason, for the reality of suffering, if we are to discover why it exists.

Countless good-hearted souls are sincere in their desires to want a more peaceful world to the benefit of everyone. Around the world, non-profit spiritual and secular organizations exist for the purpose of alleviating or ending suffering as we know it, whether it be from a catastrophic event large scale, such as a tsunami or an earthquake, or a small scale, such as homelessness in a small town.

Although there is such a strong desire to eradicate suffering on this planet, the Buddha exclaimed, "All life **is** suffering." In fact, the first of the Buddha's four noble truths is an acknowledgement that suffering exists. To be alive is to suffer. No one is immune to this aspect of our world. It is inevitable. All activity on this planet occurs due to the interplay of opposites (young – old, wealth – poverty, pleasure – pain). Happiness and enjoyment of worldly objects and events simply could not exist without the opposite experiences of sadness and pain. It is incredible to contemplate that we need unpleasant experiences to enjoy the pleasurable ones! What a life this is!! There must be some purpose, some reason for the reality of suffering if we are to discover why it exists.

The quotation by Annamalai Swami addresses a topic that has been discussed for many years by writers, theologians, and spiritual teachers. Eckhart Tolle, in his classic book, *The Power of Now*, states that without suffering, many, or perhaps most of us would contentedly live out our days, enjoying what life has to offer, but would never make a concerted attempt to pursue God. Viewed from this perspective, suffering becomes the impetus to escape the limitations of transient, worldly existence in the pursuit of the more Eternal reality, life without suffering, consisting of everlasting love and bliss.

Immediately the question arises as to what is wrong with simply enjoying what life has to offer. After all, enjoyment of life, called 'kama' in Sanskrit, is one of the goals of yoga! Why can't we be happy with this life we have been given rather than needing to think we have to improve it in order to search for God? One answer is that for almost all of us, the enjoyment of life – specifically, enjoyment of sense pleasures – simply does not last, and is insufficient. We are happy one minute, but not the next minute. When we are happy, we can feel good, and yet still ask ourselves, "Is that all there is?"

Enjoyment is perhaps easier when we are youthful, intelligent, attractive, wealthy, and healthy, but, inevitably there is the loss of youth, attractiveness, and, in the end, brain and bodily functioning. In the meantime, there is the all too real possibility of pain from disease, poverty, and loss of family and friends. Beauty is fleeting and wealth may bring momentary, but not lasting happiness, after we have taken the time to purchase the things that money can buy. It is an interesting fact that many people who realize that life has been good to them and have every reason to be happy experience depression more often than happiness. Such people help keep therapists busy in our private practices. And, in case some of us believe that we are happy with what life gives us, countless television and media advertisements abound to remind us that we would be much happier if we could only purchase their new products.

The simultaneous avoidance of suffering and the pursuit of joy is one of the essential drives in life as the great yoga master Paramahansa Yogananda, in his book *The Essence of Self Realization*, tells us. In response to Charles Darwin's statement that survival is the primary drive of human existence, Yogananda notes that survival is not, in itself, the only human goal. One could survive in a coma, he points out, and not be particularly happy. Therefore, mere existence is not enough. Humans also want to be consciously aware of their existence. Yet being consciously aware of existence while in the midst of constant suffering would still remain an unsatisfactory state and, in such a state, humans might prefer not to remain alive. The third drive of existence, then, is to experience the constant state of bliss, which entails the eradication of all suffering.

Thus the fundamental instinct of life, Yogananda says, is "a desire for continued, conscious existence (immortality) in a state of perpetual enjoyment." (p. 51) The Sanskrit word for these goals is 'Satchitananda,' or Sat (existence), Chit (consciousness), and Ananda (Bliss). The state of Satchitananda is the state of God or God's true nature, as Swami Shankaracharya defined many centuries ago. This state is, in fact, our true nature as well.

Yogananda took the necessity of suffering in human existence one step further. He noted that "Suffering is a reminder that the world is not our home. If it were perfect for us, how many people would seek a better one?" (p. 55) Thus, suffering appears to have at least a two-fold purpose: the motivation to pursue God, as well as a world where truly we belong.

It has often been the case that periods of intense pain precede periods of quantum leaps in spiritual growth. The great philosopher and pundit Ken Wilber movingly describes in his writings, and on the recent audiotape *"Kosmic Consciousness,"* the great suffering his wife endured while battling cancer. Ken reports that he attended to her needs, suffering and growing tremendously along with her, as she confronted her illness and finally her death. About a year after her death, he had a prolonged experience of transcendence through waking, dreaming, and sleeping, which led him to produce an important book on spirituality and consciousness.

The great spiritual teacher Nisargadatta Maharaj was in great pain in the last year of his life, dying from lung cancer. However, despite his state of deep fatigue, with which he was sometimes barely able to speak to his students, he seemed impervious to the pain. He merely witnessed it and downplayed its significance to his obviously distraught devotees. The recordings of the events in the life of St. Francis of Assisi also indicate that he suffered tremendously, but again, it seemed not to affect him and he accepted it as gift from God.

It is remarkable to think that some of the greatest beings the planet has known have not only undergone intense, almost unimaginable suffering, but have actively sought it out. In the West, we know well about Christ's passion and death on the cross at the hands of the Romans: a crucible he willingly accepted. Suffering so moved the Buddha that he left his posh life behind, discarded everything he loved, and sought to attain the permanent state of Nirvana - the end of all suffering. He then urged us to find time to be with those who suffer. This attitude not only evokes compassion and love, but helps us to move beyond our own suffering to culture and cultivate transcendence. Mahatma Gandhi was repeatedly imprisoned and went on long hunger strikes that left him emaciated in his quest to free India. St. Katherine Drexel was born to a wealthy and prominent Philadelphia family. She renounced her rich worldly life, giving away huge sums of money to do God's work in creating new schools for Native Americans and African American children.

The first author discovered, or, more accurately, fell upon the science of yoga and the pursuit of spirituality as the direct result of suffering. I found that coping with the stressors of demanding clinical work in an inner-city hospital while receiving a very small financial stipend to be a stressful situation. At the same time, my doctoral dissertation defense was going poorly, and I was faced with the possibility of not receiving my degree, which meant that eight years of graduate study could go up in smoke. While some may question whether this situation involved suffering, I certainly experienced it in that way. I felt I truly needed Divine intervention if I was going to complete my doctoral program, persist through a demanding internship, and find suitable employment. Thus, I opened to the possibility that a spiritual pursuit may be needed in my life if I was to succeed, and I started to pursue yoga in a serious manner.

Given that each of us will experience suffering, some more and some less, the question arises: what is the best way to deal with suffering? At one time or another each of us has tried fighting it, resisting it, running away or avoiding it, and even ignoring it. Many people try to spend their way out of suffering by purchasing various material items to reduce painful feelings. We buy new clothes, a new car, stereo equipment, or a summer home. Some people try to self-soothe through the addictive balms of alcohol, recreational drugs, sex, gambling, or the Internet. All of these well-intentioned plans sooner or later turn out to be ineffectual means for dealing with suffering. The fact of the matter is that as almost as soon as we acquire some new desirable item, we tire of it, and want something else. Nothing is ever enough. People with alcohol addictions have been found to say, 'One drink is both too many and never enough.'

Although it is counterintuitive, each of us is called, sooner or later, to embrace suffering from a spiritual dimension -- to learn from it, to look at it in a new light. According to the great seers, suffering contains the hidden seeds of God, and can wake us up to our wholeness. Suffering can motivate us. It can challenge our assumptions about life. It can purify us. It may be necessary, though unwanted.

More important than the fact that we are suffering is how we respond to our suffering. How we interpret and react to our suffering makes all the difference in terms of how much we can profit from it. Many spiritual teachers recommend acceptance as the primary method for dealing with suffering. Acceptance means simply allowing the situation to be as it is, without fighting it, denying it, or trying to change it. For example, in *The Power of Now*, Eckhart Tolle wrote extensively on how a complete acceptance of or merging with the feeling of pain as it is can be a gateway toward experiencing the bliss that is always present in the experience of the Now.

As we learned in the last lesson on awakening from fear, suffering can wake us up to our true Self -- or it can leave us bewildered, angry, despairing, and bitter, cut off from God. During times of suffering, it is essential to remember that suffering is not the true nature of life. As the great teacher Maharishi Mahesh Yogi said, suffering is a distortion of the nature of life. Many great spiritual traditions agree -- the nature of life is bliss, not suffering -- **Satchitananda.** Someone once asked Maharishi Mahesh Yogi if Jesus Christ suffered. Maharishi's response indicated that Christ may not have suffered -- that he had transcended suffering through his passion. One thing appears certain, however. Suffering can lead to growth and development, and as consciousness expands, sorrow can wane and even cease -- we can become impervious to it. The Buddha said that all suffering is caused by desire, and he encouraged us, admonished us, to eradicate our desires and be free. When we are free, we live in a world that is different than the one in which we were born. It is not that we need to leave planet earth – we can live in this world, but not be of this world – but that we need to create a heaven on earth.

A Hasidic saying states that nothing bad happens that God imposes on us. This seems to imply that we should not interpret pain and suffering in our lives negatively – the situation or event which leads us to experience suffering may be a gift from God. If we knew the big picture – our karmic map - we might readily understand how a specific situation has been sent to us for our higher benefit. In the experience of the second author (David), I saw my mother suffer horribly from lupus when I was a young boy growing up. All I know is that it hurt me deeply, and I wanted to take her pain away, but I could not. In my opinion, suffering requires acceptance -- and I accept the fact that I will always remember her suffering, even though I experience momentary pain as I recall it. After many years of spiritual practice, the pain is less intense, does not last as long, and I have learned to move from a painful state into a more easeful one.

There is a growing scientific literature on the effectiveness of spiritual practices in reducing pain. Recent research indicates that practicing yoga helps breast cancer patients feel less fatigued and more vital following therapy. Chandwani and her colleagues (2014), reporting in the Journal of Clinical Oncology, studied breast cancer patients (stages 0-3) who were given hatha yoga classes three times per week for six weeks prior to receiving radiotherapy. Patients who received yoga therapy had greater increases in vitality compared to patients on a wait list up to three months following radiotherapy. In addition, the yoga therapy group showed increases in physical functioning for up to 6 months compared to patients on a wait list, or who did stretching exercises. Yoga therapy was also associated with reduction in fatigue following therapy.

Practitioners of mindfulness-based interventions (such as Mindfulness Based Stress Reduction and Acceptance and Commitment Therapy) have been found to reduce their experiences of pain. Reiner and his associates (2013) reviewed journal articles from 1960-2010, studying the effectiveness of mindfulness-based meditation on pain intensity. Three qualities of mindfulness meditation were taught: 1) observing the reality of the present moment; 2) attending to a single aspect of immediate experience without judgment; and 3) maintaining an attitude of opening to whatever arises from inner experience. A total of 16 studies with over 1400 participants were included in the final review. These studies involved at least six hours of mindfulness meditation instruction. In six of eight controlled studies of adult pain patients, mindfulness-based interventions led to significant reductions in pain intensity. In several of the studies, the positive effects were found to last from three months to three years, which suggests long-lasting effects of mindfulness-based therapies. While a number of the studies contained nonspecific pain groups, at least three of the studies were specifically for patients with fibromyalgia, which indicates that mindfulness-based interventions may be particularly helpful for that group of pain patients. The authors hypothesized that mindfulness interventions assisted the pain patients through increasing self-acceptance, and enhancing self-regulation of behavior.

The Yoga Sutras and other great spiritual texts tell us that, as we advance on the spiritual path, our orientation to pain and sorrow—the nature of suffering—changes radically. Some texts go so far as to say that all suffering ceases. It has been our experience that by engaging in spiritual practices, the intensity of suffering diminishes over time. In addition, the resolution comes more quickly, so that after brief periods of suffering we more quickly return to a blissful state. The inevitability of suffering is followed, like the day follows night, by the development of a more frequent state of contentment, joy, and bliss. As Meister Eckhart has reminded us: "Truly, it is in darkness that one finds the light, so when we are in sorrow, then this light is nearest to all of us."

Contemplation

1. The philosopher Alan Watts said that man suffers because of his craving to possess and forever hold on to things which are essentially impermanent. This is attachment. This is clinging. This is a lack of acceptance. Take a few minutes and examine your own life, and write down what it is that you're attached to. Perhaps you could arrange these things in order of priority, from top to bottom.
2. Think of the sufferings in your life. What are the major lessons you have learned from your suffering and pain? Has your suffering caused you to consider or reconsider your relationship with God?
3. According to the science of Ayurveda, suffering occurs when we violate the laws of nature through improper diet, behavior, thinking, feeling, etc. Examine your life with a focus on the

laws of nature you believe you have consistently broken. Have you found that you reap what you sow?

4. There are many people who suffer from trauma, but simply complain about it, without trying to overcome it. In his book 'The Body Keeps the Score,' Bessel Van Der Kolk, M.D., reports on a study of trauma survivors from the Sept 11, 2001 accident at the Twin Towers in New York City. Survivors noted that acupuncture, massage, yoga, and EMDR (Eye Movement Densitization and Reprocessing), in that order, were most helpful in overcoming their traumatic experiences. Most of these treatments are nonverbal therapies. If you experience suffering due to trauma, what treatment could you try that you have not yet attempted?
5. It has been said that much suffering is simply 'resistance' to acceptance of the present moment. In other words, suffering is an attempt to undo, deny, or otherwise block the experience of what is happening in the present moment. Can you identify a time in which you have created suffering for yourself in this manner?

Application

1. Sit quietly, allow your attention to settle your breathing, and allow your mind to become calm and receptive... now allow your mind to focus on some suffering in your life -- notice how this focus affects your body, heart, and mind. Then ask yourself the following:
   - How have I addressed this problem so far?
   - Have I resisted it? How have I resisted it? What has been the effect of this resistance?

- » What does the suffering ask me to detach from, let go of, and transcend?
- » Can I let go of the suffering, offering it up to God?
- » What lesson can I learn from the suffering?
- » Realistically, what can I do about this suffering?

Now quietly and patiently listen for the answers from your heart and spirit....

2. Over the next 24 hours, engage in mindfulness meditation or another meditation practice. As you have just done, allow your mind to focus on your pain and suffering. Perhaps there is a painful spot in your body that you notice. For a short period of time, allow the pain to be present in your body without trying to resist it or remove it. Allow yourself to let go of your pain and enter into it, and be one with it. Write down your experiences or discuss with another individual when you are finished.
3. Much of our suffering becomes self-imposed by keeping negativity alive in our thoughts, words, and actions. One common way many of us keep suffering alive is through complaining. When we engage in complaining, we may unwittingly spread our negativity to those who listen to us. Try to go for a day, a week, or a month without complaining to others. Notice if there is a difference in your thoughts, mood, and attitude toward life.
4. Take every opportunity to notice things in your life that bring even the slightest iota of joy. Notice them. Magnify them. Discuss them. Suffering can be reduced when we engage in its opposite experience: joy. Find joy in the smallest of things, particularly in nature: the sound of a baby cooing, the beauty

of a puppy or rabbit playing, a flower blooming. Imbibe these sites and sounds, and allow them to remain on your mind.

5. Interview three other people, and find out how they view and have dealt with great suffering in their lives.

Lesson Five

ON DEATH

• • • • •

Illumination

"It is beautiful over there..."

Thomas Edison's last words.

Thomas Edison, 1847-1931, was known as the wizard of Menlo Park for his prolific inventions and numerous patents. He was a leader in developing generating stations to provide electric power to cities and towns all over the world, and was the founder of the General Electric (GE) company.

"... death is not extinguishing the light: it is putting out the lamp because the Dawn has come."

Rabindranath Tagore

Tagore, 1861-1941, from Bengal, India, was a monumental painter, writer, and poet, who became the first non-European to win the Nobel Prize in Literature. He was the founder of Visva-Bharati University. He travelled the world, denouncing nationalism and advocating respect and cooperation among countries.

Examination

"Death and taxes," my father would tell me, are the only two certainties in life. Seizing the career-related ramifications of this truism, my father took a job working for the IRS, rather than working as a mortician. He thought work as an IRS agent better suited his temperament.

As much as many people fear the IRS, it seems that all organisms fear death. Freud thought that the fear of death was the most basic of all fears, underlying all experiences of anxiety. Although we do know something about the dying process, there is all too little information about death in popular culture. This is not surprising, as our culture avoids images of old age whenever possible, so discussions of death are not easy to come by. If you look at the covers of the monthly AARP magazine, you will find the people depicted appear younger than they did only a few years ago. Images of older persons closer to death are definitely not 'hot.'

Usually when we do not know about something, we fill the void with our own ideas. Everybody has their own projected ideas about what death is and what the experience of it might be. For many it is the fear of nothingness -- the state of non-being. We may believe we will simply no longer exist. But is it really so? As the above quotes indicate, life after death may be a beautiful experience... and not a loss at all! The fact that many traditions and religions worldwide contain a belief in reincarnation – meaning after the soul leaves earth, it returns to earth at a later time in another form – suggests the permanence of the soul, and argues against a position of non-being. From this point of view, death is not 'real' in the sense of being permanent, but it is an 'illusion' that life has ended. Just as a caterpillar may fear 'death,' the rest that is experienced during the chrysalis stage is simply part of the transition into the freedom and beauty of the butterfly stage.

The continuing existence of the soul following death of the physical body on earth is an integral aspect of the concept of reincarnation. This is a pervasive belief in Hindu and Buddhist philosophy, and a cornerstone of ancient Egyptian and Greek philosophies. In *The Tibetian Book of the Dead*, it is explained that the individual does not reincarnate immediately after death, but first passes through three stages called 'Bardos.' The first, called Chikkhai bardo, entails the soul's viewing the "clear light of reality" at the time of death. Perhaps it was knowledge of this stage that prompted Edison to remark about the beauty on the other side. The second stage, Chonyid bardo, is the time in which the soul sees the Buddha in different forms. In the third stage, Sidpa bardo, the soul is reborn. The Greek philosophers Socrates, Pythagoras, and Plato incorporated reincarnation in their teachings, showing that a belief in reincarnation moved from Asia and into Europe.

The circumstances under which a soul reincarnates is dependent upon the 'karma' of an individual. Karma is the law of effect. All humans are subject to its law, which essentially is 'as you sow, so shall you reap,' or 'whatever goes around, comes around.' The events an individual experiences throughout life are based upon karma from previous lifetimes. Those who performed primarily good actions in a prior life are likely going to experience more favorable circumstances in the current life, relative to an individual who performed primarily negative actions. The principle of karma explains why each of us is born into and lives through different circumstances than others. We reincarnate to experience the effects of karma obtained in prior lifetimes. (An excellent book on this topic is *What Becomes of the Soul After Death* by Swami Sivananda.)

One example of evidence of reincarnation is demonstrated in the selection of the highest monk, or lama, in Tibetian Buddhism: the Dalai Lama (which means Ocean of Wisdom). The Dalai Lama is selected or found during childhood as a reincarnated soul, based upon several signs and tests, including his ability to identify possessions that were dear to him in the previous incarnation on earth. After leaving the earth at the time of death, the Dalai Lama is typically reborn in Tibet within two to three years. A search committee, including senior Lamas and government officials, are given the task to identify him when he is reborn. If a child is thought to be the reincarnated Dalai Lama, he is tested in various ways before the decision is made as to whether he is the true Dalai Lama. One test involves presenting the child with a number of articles. If the child can correctly identify those that were used in his previous life, it is a strong sign that he is the reborn Dalai Lama. The current Dalai Lama – there have been 14 of them – was identified at two years of age!

Further suggestion of the ongoing existence of the soul following death is based on reports from individuals who have survived Near Death Experiences, or NDEs. The proliferation of writers who have described their own NDEs inspires us to believe that there is life after death. Dr. Eben Alexander, M.D., Neurosurgeon, wrote of his experience traveling to heaven while in a coma for seven days in the book *Proof of Heaven.* Amazingly, after lying in a coma for seven days, Dr. Alexander regained full consciousness, was completely lucid, and wrote of his experiences in great detail. The odds against someone making such a remarkably complete recovery after seven days in a coma are more than a million to one.

Dr. Alexander wrote of travel to different worlds or spiritual realms, some terrible and terrifying, others beatific and awe-inspiring. He wrote of experiencing "an immense void, completely dark, infinite in size, yet also infinitely comforting" (p. 47). He saw countless universes containing abundant life with intelligences far in excess of human intelligence, in which love, not evil, was dominant. Interestingly, Dr. Alexander wrote that his greatest challenge after returning to waking consciousness was adequately describing the profound feeling of unconditional love. He realized that the left hemisphere of the brain, the rational, logical side of the brain, forms a barrier to the experience of pure love. The experience of unconditional love, then, must be an experience of the right hemisphere of the brain, as reported by Dr. Jill Bolte Taylor.

Perhaps the largest scientific study of NDEs has been undertaken by Jeffrey Long, M.D., and reported in his book *Evidence of the Afterlife* (2010). His study is based upon researching over 1300 NDEs from people all over the world, of various religious traditions. Dr. Long found nine commonalities in all of these experiences: Crystal Consciousness, Realistic Out-of-Body Experiences, Heightened Senses, Consciousness during Anesthesia, Perfect Playback, Family Reunions, Children's Experiences,

Worldwide Consistency, and Aftereffects. Reviewing the reports from numerous NDEs, it is clear that individuals find the experience remarkably beautiful and moving: many individuals did not want to return to earth.

Although many of us do not understand death, major religions counsel us to think about death, and not avoid it. Buddhists are encouraged to think of their death on a daily basis during meditative practices. Roman Catholics have Ash Wednesday. Once per year, prior to Lent, Catholics visit churches where priests anoint their foreheads with ash to remind them of their transient existence on earth (... "unto dust we shall return").

There are religious and spiritual systems which teach that death can bring about a significant transformation. Sogyal Rinpoche, the great Buddhist teacher, says that death, the temporal, gives way to the eternal aspect of man. Likewise, the Bodo called death a temporary end, a freeing, and a return to our original unity. Yet other traditions and teachers have counseled that death brings reward (heaven) or punishment (hell), depending upon the deeds and conduct the individual has shown on earth. For example, Paramhansa Yogananda taught that after death the "ego sense," the basic tendencies of a person's personality remain intact and guide, in a sense, where in the astral world a person will be attracted (*The Essence of Self-Realization*, pp 88-89). After spending a period in an astral world, the desires constituting the ego sense compel the individual to return to earth, in order that they may be fulfilled.

There is no room for fear of any kind on a spiritual path, and this includes fear of death. Thus, one of the great gifts that the pursuit of spiritual endeavors can provide us with is overcoming this often well-ingrained fear.

Various sages and spiritual Masters have encouraged us to understand more about death as part of our spiritual work. Advice regarding the importance of understanding death was given by the ancient Greeks. Shortly before his own death, Plato recommended that his disciples "practice dying," as a method to better understand life and death. Maharaj Nisargadatta, the great Hindu Saint, encouraged us to go to the state prior to consciousness, our original nature before our current incarnation. He felt it was necessary for our understanding to return to that state during our lifetime, and if we did, we would lose our fear of death. In Zen Buddhism, a monk may be given a koan, which encourages him or her to explore our original nature before our parents conceived us. Through this process, the fear of death can be extinguished.

When we know who and what we are, we realize that we never can really die -- only our physical bodily structures can pass away. When Tagore writes of the lamp being put out, he is referring to the death of the ego or small self, which must be extinguished to make way for the soul to identify with the light of the Great Self, referred to as the Dawn.

Throughout history, there have been those who have extolled death, although there is clearly not unanimity regarding what happens immediately after humans leave this world. Mozart called death "the truest friend of mankind." He saw death as the time when all truth is revealed. The great writer Herman Hesse referred to death as the "call of love." Thanatologist and physician Eliazabeth Kubler-Ross said that death is "simply a shedding of the physical body." She noted that the feeling of 'I amness' lives on. The great poets Whitman and Tennyson described death as beautiful and bright. Plato referred to death as the greatest of blessings! Epictetus described death as a mask, a covering.

Many of the wise discuss the relevance of the little deaths which occur each day in life -- the small and the great losses we experience with some regularity. They tell us that all of these little deaths prepare us for the great death at the end of our lives, and teach us to really surrender and let go. One theme that constantly runs through all of the wisdom accumulated by the great seers indicates that death is not real -- only apparent.

A reporter once asked Dr. Deepak Chopra if he was ever "here before" -- referring to the possibility of his reincarnation. His immediate response was interesting. He said, "We're all here all the time." He is referring to the omnipresence and eternity of being. He is referring to the Self, or what Christians might consider the soul. The soul was never born; hence, it can never die.

An individual who is established in Self-Awareness or Self-Realization has a profoundly different view of death than most of us. This individual may even welcome death. In his book *Does Death Really Exist*, Swami Muktananda quotes from the Hindu Scripture, the Bhagavad Gita, on death.

"Just as a man casts off worn-out clothes and gets new ones, so the Self casts off worn-out bodies and enters into new ones."

Commenting on this passage, Muktananda says, "When this is the case, why does one worry? Why does one weep? For a wise person, death is beautiful; it is only when one lacks knowledge that one fears it" (p. 5). Muktananda's comment suggests to us the wisdom of gaining Self-knowledge; for one of the many benefits of this wisdom is losing the fear of death.

As odd as this may sound, an individual who knows the Self may, in fact, welcome death. In the process of overcoming fear of death, one learns that what we consider 'death,' which is basically the end of our individual existence, is not real. Many spiritual teachers remind us that what we consider 'death' is an illusion. That is, what is truly real about our existence never dies; it simply changes form.

Recently, a fellow yogi, who has practiced for over 20 years, mourned the death of the Rock 'N Roll idol, Prince. She listened ardently to his music since she was a young girl. In fact, she had over 1000 of his songs on her cell phone. For weeks she was distraught. Then, one day, after listening to a sacred mantra playing on You Tube, all of her grief went away in a flash. But, even more surprisingly, so did her fear of death. She realized that she would be just as content whether she was alive or dead; therefore, death had no grip over her mood, or internal state. Overcoming the fear of death is one of the many gifts of participating in spiritual practices.

Contemplation

1. Look back on your life and call to mind all of your experiences with death: the death of loved ones, the death of pets, even the death of plants and flowers. What have your experiences with death taught you? What are your associations with death, and how do they affect you in your day-to-day life?
2. What do you honestly know about death? What are your fears? What do you think happens at the time of death? Why do you think so many wise persons say similar things about death?
3. If you question whether life begins at birth and ends at death, ask yourself, when did you become a conscious being? Were

you conscious while in the womb? If so, where did your consciousness come from? Was it a byproduct of the meeting of the egg and ovum? Or did you become conscious at your time of birth? If you did, where did that consciousness come from? From where have you derived your capacity to love, to experience awe, to have the interests and talents that you have? Do they all come from your DNA? If so, are all your abilities due to random alignments of DNA, created shortly after the moment of conception? Were those alignments purely random??

4. What would be your last prayer to God at the moment of your death?
5. Chuang Tzu said that when beings return to the formlessness of death, they retain reality without place and duration without time. Take a few moments and imagine what it is like to be timeless and spaceless...

Application

1. Make an exhaustive list of all your fears concerning death. After you have done this, come up with a plan to deal with each and every one of these fears.
2. Make another list -- this time, list all the things that you are avoiding in life – again, come up with a plan to confront these situations.
3. Presume you will die within one week. Write a letter to all of your loved ones and to God, expressing your gratitude for them for how they have helped you in life. If you like, share this letter with those you love. In this way, you can complete 'unfinished business' before you depart from this world.

4. Meditation on the death experience.

   You're about to die. Try to culture a feeling of love. Say goodbye to and thank all the parts of your body -- also say goodbye to and thank your personality -- now imagine God is near. He/She is with you now. Feel God filling up your body with his love -- listen to him...

   Now imagine you're lying in state... what do you look like? Who is there? What are they saying to one another? Is there a clergyman present? What is he or she saying? Simply identify your anxieties -- your resistances -- your fears -- and note any positive experiences you're having, and delight in them. Say your goodbyes to each person in the room, and a general goodbye to all of them... as you look back at your life, what are your reflections? Allow your attention to stay with this process for a few minutes, and then return to the here and now -- how are things different?

5 – How are you preparing to die and for your life to come?

   Imagine that you can create your future in a heavenly realm. You are both the actor and the director of your future life (lives). What would you like your life to be in the next plane of existence? How are you preparing for it now? Do you think that you have no say or no control in how your life will be at the next stage? Are you living your life as if karma does not exist, and simply 'taking your chances?' Your own actions in the present moment will determine your future karmas, both in this life and in future lives. Are you as conscious of all your thoughts and actions in each moment as you need to be, in preparation for your future life to come?

Lesson Six

ON SPIRITUALITY

• • • • •

Illumination

"We are not human beings having a spiritual experience; we are spiritual beings having a human experience."

Pierre Teilhard de Chardin

Teilhard, 1881-1955, was a Jesuit priest and theologian who originally trained as a paleontologist and geologist. Among his many published works was the *'The Phenomenon of Man,'* which depicts the evolution of consciousness toward a psychic unity of mankind.

Examination

It is quite possible that you may be reading this book and quietly telling yourself that none of this pertains to you, because you are just not a 'spiritual person,' as if a 'spiritual person' is someone different than you, who is more holy, believes in God, or is committed to spiritual practices. Or you may simply think you are not good enough to be a spiritual person. So if you wonder if you are a 'spiritual person,' or are convinced there is no way that you are a 'spiritual person,' this chapter will likely interest you.

Allow us to try to convince you that you are, indeed, a spiritual person. These are the qualifications for being spiritual, as near as we can discern: 1) You are breathing, and 2) You are currently an inhabitant of planet earth. Obviously, you meet our loose criteria, but you may say that you have no interest in spirituality, are not good at it, or do not know what it means. Fair enough. Allow us to describe what we understand spirituality to be. First, spirituality is not religion, although for some persons, there is little or no difference. Spirituality, according to one definition, tends to be a person-centered, as opposed to God-centered, term which is "anchored in a quest for a directed, unmediated experience of the transcendent realities..." (Sperry and Shafranske, 2005, p. 17). That is, spirituality is about having direct experience with or in interaction with the Divine. It is not so much about interaction with God that is mediated by others or institutions, such as formalized churches. The present authors make no claims to have expertise in religion, and this book is clearly not about religion.

Second, by spirituality, we are speaking of who you truly are at the very core of your being. That is, we do not regard you as solely a physical person, nor do we see the physical body as the primary aspect of who you are. Third, while we know you have a mind, we do not regard the mind as the primary aspect of who you are. Your spirit, or your spirituality, refers to your soul, your connection with nature, your capacity to love and to feel love, your need and interest for intimacy with other human beings at their deepest levels, and, finally, your desire to know yourself. We should also add that no one person is inherently more spiritual than any other person. There are differences, however, among us in our awareness of who we truly are and how much attention we spend to our inner state of Oneness.

Just because you may have physical or psychological problems, addictions, poverty, loneliness, or an absence of interest in this topic means absolutely nothing about the truth of your spirituality, or your capacity to participate in and profit from spiritual pursuits. Plenty of people who have experienced pain, depression, anguish, loss, heartache, addictions, and other types of suffering have used these experiences as springboards to pursue spirituality. Simply thinking you are not spiritual does not make you less so. Moreover, you can pursue spirituality regardless of your religion. Do not think you need to alter or abandon your religious beliefs and pursuits in order to deepen your spiritual nature. Continue your religious practices exactly as you have been doing. Spiritual practices will likely enhance your understanding of and practice of your religion.

The Buddha said that man needs a spiritual life just as a candle needs a flame. According to all the great spiritual Masters, spirituality is essential. The great French Jesuit paleontologist and theologian, Teilhard de Chardin, tells us that our original nature is spirit. He said that we are spiritual beings having a human experience, not human beings having a spiritual experience. The Catholic Church tells us that we are "made in the image and likeness of God." Our very essence is spiritual. We do not have to try to be spiritual. We need only transcend the blocks, or impediments, to realizing our spirituality -- clear away the obstacles, and just let our spirituality manifest. Mother

Teresa asked, "Are we not all divine and made for a higher life?" The obvious answer is yes. Various writers have posited that human beings are at the midpoint of Consciousness as it first descends into matter (involution), and then begins its return home (evolution), back to undifferentiated oneness. Thus, all human beings are inherently spiritual.

So what is our view of spirituality? There is no single or easy definition, but we think of spirituality as the ability to be in tune with and connect to all that is, both within and outside oneself. The science and practice of spirituality has been discussed by numerous persons over the years. Recently the Dalai Lama (*Understanding Enlightenment*), Jon Kabat- Zinn (e.g., *Wherever You Go, There You Are*), and Eckhart Tolle (e.g., *The Power of Now*) have been among the numerous teachers who have popularized spiritual practices for many in the West. For the purposes of our discussion, spirituality is about personal 'connection' with or becoming attached to 'All That Is.' There are many words have been used to describe 'All That Is,' including 'Source,' 'Supreme Consciousness,' 'Self,' 'Pure Being,' and 'God,' among others. The precise words that are used to describe the 'Infinite One' are not essential, in that there are many.

The spiritual practices that we suggest fall into several areas: 1) Awareness and attention; 2) Concern and empathy; 3) Meditation; and 4) Awe, wonder, love and respect.

When we think of awareness and attention, we think of focusing these tools on our body, mind, and spirit/soul. Awareness is our ability to observe and perceive. We are aware 24 hours per day, whether we are asleep or awake, although sometimes our attention seems divided into several areas at once. We can be aware of how we are breathing, for example. Are we breathing shallowly or deeply? Quickly or slowly? Are we breathing through our nose or mouth? In a similar manner, we can be aware of how we are eating. Are we taking the time to chew our food slowly, which is an aid in our digestion, or are we trying to gulp it down as quickly as possible to rush off to an appointment? Are we aware of when our stomachs are full, and do not need more food? Are we aware of the effects of the food we are eating and the beverages we are drinking on our stomach? How does that sugary soda or fried food feel in our stomach after we have consumed it? Finally, we can be aware of how we are moving our bodies. For instance, if we are lifting an object that is too heavy, our body may send us a signal in the form of pain, so that we put the object down before we do some serious damage to a body part. We can be aware of what we are thinking. Are we thinking uplifting thoughts? Beneficial thoughts? Calming thoughts? Or are we thinking thoughts which lead to stress and anxiety? An old advertisement says that "We are what we eat," but it can also be said that we are what we think. The practice of mindfulness, the ability to sustain awareness of the present moment over a period of time, as advocated by Jon Kabat-Zinn, has been linked to improvements in psychological and physical functioning in numerous research studies. Recently, the book *Prescribing Health,* edited by David (the 2nd author) and Dr. Deborah Bevinno, describes many of the health benefits derived from practicing Transcendental Meditation. If we were to employ our innate awareness of our bodies, minds, and souls by listening to the feedback we receive, we would have far fewer physical problems. Finally, we can be aware of our experiences of stimuli outside of ourselves, such as listening to an uplifting poem or piece of music, viewing a painting, or watching a sunset.

Concern and empathy involve awareness and attention to other people and the many forms of nature. As we become aware of the effects of our actions on other people, we demonstrate our spiritual capacity. With the understanding that each of us is God in a different form, we have an opportunity to practice concern and empathy for others. According to how we treat other persons, we very much reap the consequences of our actions in the form of either good or bad karma.

Experiencing awe/wonder in connecting with that which is greater than our individual selves brings awareness of our souls, our innate spirituality. As we connect with the beauty and grandeur outside ourselves, we are immediately in touch with the infinite capacity for beauty and grandeur within ourselves. We touch that deep place within us that possesses the infinite capacity to appreciate beauty and infinite ability to love. This includes love for ourselves, love for others, love for nature, and love for all of creation.

Lastly, we turn our attention to the question of why it appears so difficult to touch and experience our innate spirituality. Sadly, most of us are acutely focused on our shortcomings, and we equate our humanness with frailty and weakness. We connect with powerless, we feel ineffectual, and our negative judgments block our ability to feel our more highly-evolved spiritual sides. It turns out that the problem is we are looking for spirituality in the wrong place! We will not find it in our personalities, in our egos, or in our thoughts. We will find it in our Higher Self. And the Self must be experienced, not simply discussed. Experiencing the Self is not cannot merely be an intellectual exercise. We must see beyond the distortions of our human nature and experience the Divinity that lies at our core. The analogy here is that of a pond. When it is still and clear, we can see the bottom of the pond. But when we toss a stone into the water, the clarity is lost as the water ripples. The distortions in our perception and sensations are like the ripples on the surface of the water of the pond.

Through prayer, meditation, contemplation, and other spiritually-oriented activities can we quiet the incessant chatter in our minds, and appreciate our spirit in all its clarity and purity. Proverbs 20:27 says that the spirit of man is the candle of the Lord (yet, another reference to candles in spiritual literature). And the great theologian Paul Tillich boldly proclaims that Spirit is God himself. It has been said that the spirit of man is inseparable from the infinite and can be satisfied with nothing less than the infinite. According to St. Augustine, we will remain forever restless until we rest in God.

The point of this lesson is to recognize that you already are a spiritual being, a great one, just as you are. You do not need to try to become one. Utilize the spiritual capabilities you have. Do this in the smallest way possible each and every day. Smell a flower. Hug a child. Stare at a tree and rock. Feel your connection to these things and in your actions. It will not be long before your connectedness to other persons, to nature, and to your soul deepens and strengthens.

Contemplation

1. Spirituality is derived from the Latin word spiritus, which means breath or breathing. Who or what is responsible for the fact that we are breathing? In other words, contemplate 'Who is it that breathes?' Notice how effortless your breathing

is, and how uncomfortable you are without it! Consider that each breath you take is a gift for you, the gift of life.

2. Imagine that you have no beliefs about what spirituality is, or that none of your existing beliefs are of much value in pursuing spirituality. This is not because your beliefs are incorrect, but because the experience of 'The Infinite Source' is beyond all beliefs.
3. Under what conditions do you feel most spiritual? How do you feel when you're out in nature, walking in the woods, meadows, or in the mountains? How do you feel gazing at a baby? How do you feel learning about mass killings? Each of these feelings can be considered spiritual.
4. Can you distinguish mundane thoughts and feelings from spiritual experiences? What spiritual experiences have you had in your life? Sometimes profound spiritual experiences are subtle; they are not necessarily fireworks, exploding in your conscious awareness.
5. What have you learned from your religion about spirituality, and how you can experience God within yourself? What practices have you been taught that can put you in touch with God on a routine basis? Is it possible to be in touch with God 24 hours per day? How might you do this?

Application

1. Go into your own backyard or to the local woods. Sit down and gaze at a tree. Simply look at it for a few minutes. Does it do anything? Does it have a purpose? Does it have any goals? Notice its shape, its contour, its surface, and its color. Notice its beauty. Similarly, sit near a body of water, such as a stream,

river, or ocean. Notice your feeling. Why do you suppose so many people want to live on the water, and pay a lot of money to do so?

2. Walk into a church, temple, or mosque. Notice what happens. What difference do you notice in your thoughts and feelings and physical sensations? Sit quietly in a spiritual place and become aware of the effect of the environment on your awareness. Contrast this feeling with the one you receive when you walk into a crowded department store. How do you feel differently? What is responsible for the difference in how you feel in these two environments?
3. Religion comes from the Latin word religare, which means to bind back, to reconnect, to relink. What do you think is getting reconnected through religious practice? The ego or self is united with God. Spirituality comes from the word meaning to breathe. Without breathing, we do not have a life. What do you see as the relationship between spirituality and religion? Discuss the distinctions and similarities with three different people.
4. Breathing meditation—an ancient meditation, aimed at unifying attention and consciousness—involves counting the breaths.

   Sit comfortably for one to two minutes. Relax and breathe easily, comfortably, and naturally. Breathe in from your abdomen. To help you with this, imagine a balloon inside your stomach, slowly filling up as you breathe in. As you inhale, count the number 'one'. As you exhale, count the number 'two'. Continue this until you get to the count of 10, and then go back to one. Have the idea during this meditation practice that there is nowhere for you to go, nothing for you to do. Allow your attention to be freed from the tethers of your thoughts. Allow your mind to slow down. If your mind wanders off in thought, gently bring it back to the breath: do not fight thoughts. Just stay with this simple breath counting for 15 to 20 minutes, and then resume your normal activity.

5. What does your spirit feel like?

Lesson Seven

ON AWAKENING: FIRST GLIMPSES OF THE SELF

● ● ● ● ●

Illumination

"When a man awakens, he finds that he is part of the one great reality, and he realizes his union with all things..."

Swami Paramananda

Paramananda, 1884-1940, was a student of Swami Vivekananda, the first Swami from India to teach in America. He became a monk before the age of 18. He founded the Vedanta Centre in Boston and lectured around the world for 34 years, until his death.

Examination

In this chapter, we discuss what it means to reach our full potential, our own highest level of awareness. As spiritual beings, we recognize that our powers and capabilities are unlimited, and we understand that we have a great destiny.

The sage Paramananda tells us that we reach this full potential when we awaken. The use of the term "awaken" to describe the highest spiritual attainment is more often used in Eastern Philosophy and Religion, and may be unfamiliar and awkward for us Westerners. Is Paramananda suggesting we are not awake? If you are reading this chapter, are you not fully awake? When the saints and sages speak of "Awakening" (or similar terms, such as "Enlightenment" or "Self-Realization"), they mean something quite different compared to our everyday usage of the word.

Awakening refers to a radical change in consciousness, which leads to an equally radical change in how we see and relate to ourselves and the world around us. The Saints and Sages throughout the ages have suggested that we live in the world ignorant of our true nature or full potential, as if we are sleepwalking. They do not mean that we are essentially asleep 24 hours per day, or are literally sleepwalking. It may be hard for us to imagine that we live in ignorance or as if we are asleep, particularly for those of us involved in efforts to improve our state of consciousness, such as receiving some form of counseling or psychotherapy, or participating in courses on self-knowledge. How can we be asleep, we wonder, when we make such great efforts to be fully 'aware?'

When the great Masters describe us as asleep, they mean that we proceed through our daily activities in a kind of trance, unaware of our full faculties and powers. By asleep, the Masters also mean we lack the knowledge of our true Self, our own highest level of Being. It is clear that the ancient Greeks placed a high value on this form of knowledge. Inscribed at the entrance to the ancient Greek Temple to Apollo at Delphi are two words: “Know Thyself.” These words described what the ancients considered the most important task each human should strive to accomplish. Plato wrote various books in which Socrates repeatedly recommended that his followers to follow this dictim, lest they acquire false knowledge of themselves derived from public opinion, or before they sought knowledge from other (false) sources.

What does it mean to awaken? Normally, when we awaken each morning, we are no longer asleep. We are in a different state of conscious awareness. We are fully aware of the external world, and are neither in a state of deep sleep nor dreaming. We have shifted our awareness from a world that is presumably not real – the dream world – to the world of outer reality. We achieve complete awareness of our external world when we awake. But, to the Masters, the external world in which we function is a dream world, a world marked by delusion. To the Masters, the external world is every bit as much a dream world as is the world of dreams we experience at night. The delusion regarding the reality of the external world is the product of the limited ego, or limited sense of “I-ness.” We believe ourselves to be fully encased in the physical body, separate from others, and to have limited capabilities. We believe that each man/woman is an island, and, therefore, we often fear loneliness. The Masters constantly encourage us to awaken from the delusion of the external world, and overcome our primary identification with being a separate individual existing only in a physical body.

Although terms such as “Awakened” and “Enlightened” are used interchangeably, we prefer the term “Self-Realization.” An examination of the term ‘Self’ suggests that as we awaken, we embody our true nature: who we truly are at the highest level of reality. We attain our true identity with 'All that Is.' We don't become anyone else, or someone we are not. According to the Merriam-Webster dictionary, the word 'realize' means to become aware of, or cause something to become real. Putting these words together indicates that as we wake up to the state of Self-Realization, we become fully aware of our true nature, or true identity. This term also suggests that, rather than a transient 'state,' Self-Realization is a permanent condition. As awakened beings, we live in the constant awareness of who we truly are, and, at the same time, leave behind the delusion, or misguided understanding, of who we thought we were: the delusion of a limited isolated individual, residing only in the external world.

For many reasons it is extremely difficult to write about the state of Self-Realization. The Great Beings have made it abundantly clear that the state of Self-Realization cannot be described in words or comprehended by the mind. It is a state beyond the senses as well as beyond words, thought, feelings, or imagination. The only way to understand the state of Awakening is to personally experience it. One cannot describe the highest state any more readily than one can describe the external world to one who is blind, or the taste of honey to one bereft of taste buds.

So why write about the state of Self-Realization if we cannot describe it? Isn't this hypocritical? The reason is that we have been reminded repeatedly by numerous great souls that the state of Self-Realization is our very birthright. We took birth to attain this state. It is the very essence of who we are. It is a state in which all of our longings are fulfilled. Is this not worth trying to discover? We write about the state of Self-Realization because, to pursue it, we have to start somewhere. Any knowledge regarding the goal of human existence can help motivate or propel us to seek it, every bit as much as the experience of suffering, described in the previous chapter, motivates us to find it. The pursuit of Self-Realization is the single most important task we can accomplish while walking on this Earth.

Fortunately, a number of individuals (admittedly a small segment of the population) have given us glimpses into the nature of this state. At this time, it appears that more and more people are experiencing genuine spiritual awakenings. For example, in two of her earliest books (*When Fear Falls Away* and *The Freedom of Being*), author Jan Frazier writes about her own experience of awakening. She points out that when one becomes free of the ego or egoic-mind, there is no individual self; therefore, there is no one to maintain, protect, or enhance. As a result, your feelings can never be hurt, and you are never subject to others' opinions of you. You become free from all fear. She adds, "... there is almost a childlike delight in living, a perennial freshness of encounter... The capacity for fun, for spontaneity, for carefree engagement with whatever life delivers is boundless" (*The Freedom of Being*, p. 42).

Neuroanatomist Jill Bolte Taylor described an experience of 'awakening' after sustaining a massive stoke in her TED talk 'Stroke of Insight,' available on YouTube. (Her talk is the 2nd most frequently watched among TED talks.) While it is not clear that she lives in a permanent state of Self-Realization, she spoke of losing awareness of the left hemisphere of the brain, and having access only to the right hemisphere. The left hemisphere, she noted, processes experience in a linear manner, a succession of events connected in time. The right hemisphere, by comparison, processes information simultaneously, "all at once," and allows us to focus exclusively on the present moment. While having a stroke, she learned that the left hemisphere is responsible for our experience of separateness from others. In contrast, when processing only through the right hemisphere, she acquired a very different understanding. She discovered that we are all "energy beings connected to each other." She learned that, in the present moment – the awareness of the right hemisphere – "we are perfect, we are whole, and we are beautiful." She also noted, "We are the light-force power of the universe." Other words she used to describe her experience were "beautiful," "Nirvana," and "silent euphoria." (It is important to note that most persons who have undergone awakening have not had adverse cerebral accidents, such as strokes, but were physically intact, and otherwise healthy individuals.)

Andrew Newberg, M.D., and Mark Waldman report on data collected from 2000 individuals who responded to a web-based survey* regarding their experience of 'Enlightenment.' These researchers abstracted five characteristics of persons who genuinely considered themselves to be enlightened:

"1) A sense of unity and connectedness; 2) An incredible intensity of experience; 3) A sense of clarity and new understanding in a fundamental way; 4) A sense of surrender or loss of voluntary control; and 5) A sense that something – one's belief, one's life, one's purpose – has suddenly and permanently changed" (Newberg & Waldman, 2016, p. 53).

A fully awakened or enlightened soul may not be readily recognized while out in public. In fact, an individual who has 'awakened' may have exactly the same life circumstances as she did prior to awakening. Awakened individuals have been rich and poor, young and old, kings and servants. The great Indian Poet Saint, Tukaram Maharaj, for example, was a cobbler. To the awakened individual, the particular life circumstances into which he was born do not in any way affect his moment to moment experience of the joy of living. Thus there is no need to change anything about outer life circumstances.

An inability to adequately convey the nature of the highest state in words is only one of a number of paradoxes involving the state of being 'Awakened.' Another paradox is that we do not need to become better or more perfect human beings to reach the state of Self-Realization. In other words, attaining this state is not about acting sufficiently humble, charitable, nice, or "saintly." Furthermore, reaching this state may not require years of self-improvement or psychotherapy. We do not need to correct or eliminate our personality foibles and flaws.

Still another paradox is that the state of awakening does not demand the passage of time. For some, it has occurred instantaneously, in no time at all. Self-realization may not require arduous spiritual practices for a specified number of hours or years before we are 'certified.' The Great Beings remind us that the state of perfection exists in this very moment, right now, and will not be attained in some faraway indefinite future after we will have paid our dues. All this is not to deny that spiritual practices are very important, and that over a period of time, many persons make great progress as a result of their practice, and move toward a 'ripeness' or readiness for a spiritual awakening. Each person walks his or her own path, and there may be no way for us to know what will be required of us in terms of how much to practice, or what types of practices to perform before we 'awaken.'

> We do not need to become better or more perfect human beings to reach the state of Self-Realization.

Some of the great Beings have written that we really do not evolve or develop -- we only awaken. But what do we wake up to? We wake up to our original nature, as Zen puts it. Currently, when you wake up in the morning, your consciousness becomes aware of the everyday (delusional) reality. When you are 'Awake', you are permanently established, in a state described as 'unity consciousness.'

For many, spiritual awakening seems to unfold in a gradual, progressive process. However, as we proceed along a spiritual path and engage in spiritual practices, a phase shift can happen. Awareness expands; it clarifies, it deepens. This is not an achievement or an attainment -- it is rather an **undoing --** the veil of transitory existence and appearances falls away. The eternity behind all change is revealed, and we wake up to what really is -- we move beyond our conditioning and leave it behind. This is called Satori in Zen Buddhism. The person who is awake is a self-aware individual. He is free. He is his own person. He is independent. The great Buddhist psychologist Jack Kornfield tells us that we are the reality we are seeking, that we are who we are waking up to. And, as the Upanishads tell us, "The seeker is the sought."

There is merit in distinguishing between those persons who have had an experience or recurrent experiences of 'Awakening' – which we will call a 'Glimpse' - from those who are permanently established in the state of Self-Realization or God-Realization (or whatever term you prefer). That is, some people experience "glimpses" of the Self, as Vidya Frazier puts it in her book, *The Art of Letting Go: A Pathway to Inner Freedom*, for an ongoing period of time prior to attaining a complete trust in and identification with the Self. Vidya indicates that she experienced a number of qualities in her glimpses: love, peace, freedom, a sense of well-being, vastness, omniscience, emptiness, oneness, and knowing. After experiencing a glimpse, she writes, it is beneficial to let go of false identification with the mind, the body, the ego, the roles we play, and the stories we tell ourselves. Over time, it is necessary to surrender to the Self, through accepting life as it is and trusting that all of our needs will be provided.

In her book, entitled *How to Reach Enlightenment,* Polly Campbell enumerates three separate stages in the process of awakening. The first stage, named 'Becoming aware of life as it is,' involves an awareness of expanding our identity and interest beyond our personal accumulations of material objects and wealth. Persons in this stage sense that they are a part of something greater and begin self-inquiry, asking questions such as "Who am I?" and "What is my purpose?" At this point, there is greater meaning in everyday life. In the second stage, called 'Connecting to all that is,' the knowledge earned from self-inquiry ceases to be merely intellectual and begins to be experiential. Persons in this stage increasingly use intuition and are more aware of their emotions and the effects of their behaviors on others. Gratitude and compassion are practiced readily, and there is a dawning sense that everything occurring in the world is here to serve us. Faith flourishes during this stage. The third stage, 'Living with God,' entails the established knowledge of oneness with God. It does not need to be proven. The feeling of liberation arises when a person realizes he does not need to feel limited by the body or by beliefs. Fear disappears and there is no reason to manipulate or get ahead. One lives in her highest state, radiating light and love.

The Dalai Lama prescribes different exercises and tasks the seeker needs to accomplish to reach enlightenment. These exercises are recommended to allow the seeker to purify the mind and change the primary identification from the individual egoic self to the Great Self of All. In his book on *Enlightenment*, His Holiness the Dalai Lama describes contemplation practices that can lead to enlightenment. The contemplations are classified into the Initial Level, Middle Level, and High Level of practice. At the Initial Level, he recommends contemplations involving the recognition of our fortunate status as human beings, knowing we will die, thinking about future lives, identifying the refuge (in a true Guru and sacred scriptures), and karma. At the High Level, he recommends altruism, engendering great compassion, switching self and other, viewing reality (from the highest perspective without delusion), the way to analyze (distinguishing the limited "I" consciousness from the Great Self of All), and Buddhahood (Enlightenment).

There are many teachers and Great Beings, and each may recommend a different set of spiritual practices for their students to perform. Our journeys (David and I) have entailed being affiliated primarily with a single teacher and performing the practices recommended by that teacher. It can be overwhelming to try different practices recommended by various teachers, despite the fact that there may be great merit in all of them!

Given the information in the current chapter, right now, in this very moment, you can start by considering yourself as a Divine Being and acknowledging your Oneness with all that is. Shift your identification. Release or let go of your tendency to identify with limitation (e.g, "I am poor," "I am disabled," "I have mental health problems," "I am an addict..."). Identify with your inner greatness, not your perceived inner weakness. Recognize that it is not necessary for all of our everyday problems to be resolved or disappear before we begin this practice. Start your practice where you are and as you are, fully accepting who you are right in this present moment. It matters not who you were, what you have done, or what you identified yourself with yesterday or five seconds ago.

Contemplation

1. The great Saint Sivananda says that life is a series of awakenings. Look back on your life. Can you see any evidence of awakenings? What are they and what did they feel like? How did you change after your awakenings?
2. Papa Ramdas has said that every awakened man and woman knows that the object of life is to realize God. Can you think of a worthier or higher goal? If you agree with him, how do you think this helps you with your life direction?
3. Awakening is often preceded by intense pain and suffering. Has this happened to you? To what did you awaken after your suffering?

Application.

1. When you wake up tomorrow morning, consider: Where were you before you awoke? Did you exist? Did you think, did you believe, did you have feelings and bodily sensations? Did you have an identity? What do the answers to these questions tell you about the necessity of the mind, and the process of conditioning?

2. Imagine you got bumped on the head and forgot everything you ever learned! How would you feel? Who or what would be your identity?
3. Think of a time you had a sudden insight into a situation or problem – an "Aha!" experience. How were you different? How did it affect your attitudes, thoughts, and beliefs?
4. A meditation on perfection.

   Close your eyes. Take a relaxing breath or two. Suggest to yourself that everything is perfect exactly as it is. You are perfect. Your thoughts and feelings are perfect. Your life circumstances are perfect. Your family and friends are perfect. Anything and everything that arises in your mind, body, and being is perfect. Meditate on the feeling that arises as you consider everything in your inner and outer world as perfect.
5. The great Indian sage, Ramana Maharishi, recommended the practice of self-inquiry to many devotees who approached him with the question of how to achieve Self-Realization. He recommends meditation on the question "Who am I?" or "Where does this I come from?" (*No Mind, I Am The Self,* David Goodman 2007)

   Get in a comfortable position and close your eyes. Allow yourself to relax for a few minutes. And then gently say to yourself, "Who am I?" Perhaps I am my body. I feel with it; I move with it. I take in information through it. But I have a body. Therefore, I am not my body. Again, say, "Who am I?" Perhaps I am my mind. I am constantly thinking; my mind is constantly going... but I have a mind -- therefore I am not my mind. Maybe I am my emotions. After all, I have feelings all day long. After all, what would I be if I had no feelings? However, I have feelings -- I am not my feelings. "Who am I?"

Perhaps I am my personality, my character. I have all sorts of traits and qualities that contribute to my identity and self-concept. People know me through my personality. However, I have a personality – therefore, I cannot be my personality. "Who am I?" Well, if I am not my body, my mind, my feelings, or my personality -- I must be prior to all of these. I am the possessor of all of these. I am a witness to all. I am prior to consciousness. I simply am. I am, I am, I am. I am...

Silently repeat "I am" for about five minutes. Then slowly open your eyes.

If other thoughts arise while doing this exercise, Ramana Maharishi recommends asking, "To whom did these thoughts arise?" If the answer is "To me," you may then return to the question, "Who am I?" Repeated questioning and practice allows to mind to return to its Source (the Self), and the thoughts that have arisen will calm down. Practicing steadily over a period of time allows the mind to increase in ability to abide in the Source.

*Granted, there are numerous methodological and other questions regarding the validity of using self-report questionnaires to assess whether one is 'Enlightened.' When trying to describe who is enlightened, some of the Masters have said "it takes one to know one."

Lesson Eight

KNOWING GOD: BEING ESTABLISHED IN SELF AWARENESS

• • • • •

Illumination

"God becomes man, that man might become God..."

St. Athanasius

St. Athanasius, 296 AD – 373 AD, was Bishop of Alexandria. He was considered the greatest Catholic theologian of his time.

"We cannot get away from God, though we can ignore him..."

James E. Cabot

James Cabot, 1821-1903, was an American philosopher and author. He taught philosophy at Harvard and was a transcendentalist. He corresponded with Henry David Thoreau.

Examination

Once again, in this chapter, we discuss the final goal of spiritual pursuits. While it may seem very early in this spiritual program to discuss the end point of our work, we reiterate that it is extremely beneficial to start with our final goal in mind.

Stephen Cope, in his book *Yoga and the Quest for the True Self,* writes that after a spiritual awakening, "some of us are never the same." He adds, "We are haunted by what we have experienced. It echoes in everything we do (p. 43)." For this reason, after having a spiritual awakening or a profound experience of the Divine, there are those who seek permanent establishment in Unity with God (often referred to as "Self-Realization"). These individuals wish to continue to have profound spiritual experiences, and go on to know the complete Truth of who they are. For many, after an experience of awakening, an aspirant engages in spiritual practices over a period of time. Often these practices are carried out under the guidance of a teacher, a Master or Guru, who has attained the state of Self-Realization. The name for these spiritual practices in some Eastern traditions is 'sadhana.' In Christianity, these systematic practices have been called 'The Way.'

What if you are reading this chapter and immediately conclude, "I have never had a spiritual awakening or even a glimpse of a higher spiritual level. I cannot relate to this; what do I do?" Our best advice is to move forward as if you have had one, or more than one. Look at many of your mundane experiences as spiritual experiences or awakenings. Your ability to enjoy a candy bar, a baby, a sunset, or bathing in the ocean is a spiritual experience. Rather than believing your joy in these experiences comes from the candy, the baby, the sun, or the ocean, connect with the fact that your joy comes from within your own being, not from anything external to yourself. We implore you to please trust in yourself as a fully qualified spiritual being who has glimpses of the Truth, and awakenings to your higher nature. Listen to the words of St. Athanasius: God has become man – THAT'S YOU!!! – so that man – THAT'S YOU, again – might become God. Knowing God, merging with God, is your destiny.

In addition to reading these chapters, assimilating the teachings, and doing the exercises, you may feel your appetite has been whetted to also follow a spiritual path with a Master teacher.

Anyone and everyone can follow a spiritual path. Different spiritual paths proscribe a particular set of practices, and there is great value in systematically following the practices in one's chosen path, lest a seeker attempt some practices from tradition A, some from tradition B, and some from tradition C. Some teachers have maintained that seekers who sample practices from various spiritual traditions make less progress than if they were completely devoted to a particular path; however, there does not appear to be unanimity of agreement on this point. To become a master in any field, whether it be science, music, or art, typically requires intensive study and preparation over a long period of time. This principle also holds true in the area of spirituality, or spiritual science.

Knowing or merging with God is a challenge. God is often described as Nameless and Formless. Pursuing a challenge can be easier when we can see, feel, and touch what it is we are pursuing. Let us provide a rudimentary definition of our understanding of God for those who read this book. We subscribe to a belief that God exists equally in all living beings and also in all inanimate objects. In other words, the Supreme Being, or Supreme Consciousness, is the ground (i.e., the basis) for all that is. In other words, there is nothing that is not Supreme Consciousness. Another way to express this concept is that we are all a spark of the Divine. Humans differ, of course, in terms of how readily they identify with and radiate with the frequency of their inner Divine Being.

For those on a spiritual path seeking God-Realization, there are many ups and downs. That is, there are times of ecstasy and clarity mixed with times of depression, confusion, and despair. St. John of the Cross has described some of his personal challenges in his book "Dark Night of the Soul." He found that the closer he came to approaching God over time, the more difficult this task became. This challenge is made even more difficult when we seek to know Her as if She were an object of perception, located somewhere "out there," somewhere to be found, discovered, or retrieved. To our way of understanding, approaching God is completely different from an approach to any other goal. Understanding God requires a complete reorientation in thinking and perception. For God is not an object, not a thing. God is subject. God is pure subjectivity. God is the knower, not the known. God is that by which all is known that can be known.

God's subjectivity is described brilliantly in Meister Eckhart's expression "The eye with which I see God is the same eye by which God sees me..." The eye does not see itself, since it itself is doing the seeing! And as Percy Bysshe Shelley has said of God, He is "the eye with which the universe the holds itself and knows itself divine." Again, God is pure subjectivity, pure process.

Therefore, it can be said in a very real way that we cannot find God, for it is God who is doing the finding through us!

Because we are part and parcel of God, as the opening quote by James Cabot suggests, we can never be away from God, we can never be disconnected from him; but we can be ignorant of His presence. We can be lost in a state of lack of awareness.

Realized Beings have pointed out that it is insufficient to simply have an intellectual understanding of God, a conceptualization of the Divine. What we really need is to experience God. There no substitute for direct, personal experience. Not even the most sublime intellectual concept can begin to approach the knowledge gained through direct experience. Experiencing God requires spiritual practice for most of us -- unless we are fortunate enough to be born mystics, who, if they are to be believed, have the constant experience of the divine: the beatific vision.

Spiritual practice involves prayer, meditation, and contemplative exercises, as well as service to humankind. Yet the outcome of spiritual practice, ironically enough, entails more unlearning than learning. It requires clearing ourselves of misunderstandings, false attachments, and fruitless desires. St. John of the Cross said, “The soul has to proceed rather by unknowing rather than knowing” (Bk. 1, Ch. 4 #5). In the Sanskrit hymn, Shri Guru Gita (Song of the Guru), it is said, “He who thinks he knows, knows not.” We do not find God through dry, intellectual knowledge or through the ability to quote scripture. Rather, God is experienced in utter quiet, profound stillness (“Be still and know that I am God” – Psalm 46:10).

Science suggests that the experience of the divine involves a change in the level, or state of consciousness. Ongoing research in the field of neurotheology has demonstrated the changes associated with the subjective experience of the divine -- contact with God. We are getting closer to mapping out the neurophysiological route in the brain that subserves and mediates the experience of God. Andrew Newberg, MD, of The University of Pennsylvania, reports the results of decades of research into how the experience of Enlightenment changes the brain. He collected data on over 2000 persons who responded to a questionnaire on his website. These individuals claimed to have been enlightened, although it is unclear whether they may have had a 'glimpse' of the Self or were permanently established in Self- awareness. Nevertheless, distinct changes in both the parietal lobe and the thalamus were found among persons identifying themselves as 'enlightened.'

By clearing away the obstacles or impediments to the experience of God, any of us can achieve union and intimacy with him. In most cases, however, to do this we must purify our awareness, clarify our consciousness, and transcend our minds: that is, detach and distance ourselves from mundane, commonplace thoughts. As the great Saint Satya Sai Baba said, "God is concealed from the mind, but revealed in the heart." God is man minus his desires.

What is the best way to approach God? I believe it is innocence and humility. Start fresh, start anew. Clean the slate (this is called 'Beginners Mind' in Zen). The word 'God' is laden with associations, many of which are so negative and confusing that it's worthwhile to dispense with all of them and begin again. Don't pretend to know. Don't intellectualize God. If you haven't found Him yet, don't give up and don't think him away. Strive constantly to experience Him. Listen to the mystics of all religions. Read about them and their experiences, as those experiences can inspire us. They are calling to us across the ages. Vivekananda tells us that it is the God within your own self that is impelling you to seek Him. God is the nearest of the near -- the reality of your body and soul. God made us. We are made from Him. We are His creation, true children of God. He is as near to us as our own breath. As the great mystic Meister Eckhart said, "There where the creature ends, God begins to be." God does not ask anything of you other than you go out of yourself according to your mode as creature and that you let God be God in you.

Allow yourself to melt into God, to fuse with Him, to join with Him in the most intimate of ways. Allow His presence to emerge in you. Allow yourself realization of the Divine within you.

As Albert Einstein has indicated, God is the great intelligence of the universe, and also the realest of the real. God is, with the human mind, inconceivable, indescribable, ineffable. All of the great spiritual texts ever written echo this idea. The Upanishads say that God is the unseen behind all that is seen -- pure unity, pure peace, and bliss. Non-duality.

The great psychologist, William James, said that the spirit is infinite life and power." Benedict Spinoza said that God is the diffused Consciousness that animates the world. And what is that Consciousness? According to John 4:16 -- God is love.

Those who have attempted to describe God in words have created countless names for Him. In various scriptures, these names are sacred and divinely inspired. In Hinduism, there are 108 names for Lord Shiva and 1000 names for Lord Vishnu. The large number of names for Lord Vishnu seems to suggest that there are no limits to how one may describe and praise God. Many names for God exist in Christianity as well. In the Lord's Prayer it is said, "Hallowed be Thy name." The Lord's name is sacred: saying his name, singing his name, and even thinking his name are great spiritual practices that confer many benefits. Thus, various traditions in both the East and the West proscribe the repetition of the Name of God as a spiritual practice. Repeating God's name brings the spiritual seeker closer to God.

There are individuals who were said to have been born in a state of Self-Realization. Moses from the Old Testament and Shri Bhagavan Nityananda, a 20th century Indian saint, are two examples. But for others, after glimpses or initial awakening, permanent establishment in Self-Realization appears to occur over a period of time and practice. As the glimpses occur more and more frequently, the spiritual seeker appears to develop the ability to sustain them on a permanent basis.

Jan Frazier and Vidya Frazier, among others, describe their spiritual journeys as an ability to sustain glimpses of the Self for longer and longer periods of time; and, one day, they maintained their experience on a permanent basis, no matter what was happening in their external lives. There are perhaps innumerable ways to describe what it is like to abide permanently in the Self. Writing about Self-Realization, the Master Yogananda wrote: "... the inner light comes into clear and steady focus. The inner sounds become all absorbing. The sound of the sacred syllable AUM (pronounced 'OM' in English) fills the brain; its vibration moves down the spine, bursting open the door of the hearts' feeling, then flowing out into the body. The whole body vibrates with the sound of AUM" (p 221). Yogananda adds, "Self-Realization is the knowing in all parts of your body, mind and soul that you are now in possession of the Kingdom of God; you do not have to pray that it come to you; that God's omnipresence is your omnipresence" (p. 226).

Mathru Sri Sarada, a Self-Realized Master from the lineage of Ramana Maharishi, achieved enlightenment after four years of practice with her teacher, Sri Lakshmana. She described the state of Self-Realization in this way:

"...there was only peace inside and out. I knew that I was the Self and that when I uttered the word 'I', this 'I' meant only the Self. Even though I may see, I am not seeing: even though I may hear, I am not hearing; even though I may talk I am not talking. When I wake up I am not really waking and when I sleep I am not really sleeping. Sleep, waking and dream are passing before the Self but they cannot touch it. Whatever I may do I am not doing it. I have no sin and no virtue, no sleep and no waking, for I am always in the state of sahaja Samadhi. Whatever I may do, I am always in that state." (*No Mind, I Am the Self,* David Godman, 2007, p. 188)

Why do we, the authors, search for the Inner Self? It is simple. Spiritual glimpses of bliss, love, and freedom are simply too exquisite to take for granted. To not want to pursue them would be tantamount to throwing away or ignoring the gift of a great fortune. Our experiences tell us that, just as Ponce De Leon searched for a fountain of youth or Sir Edmund Hillary searched for the north pole, there is too much at stake not to make this journey. There is so much to gain through spiritual transformation. If we have managed to intrigue you, whetted your appetite, or opened your mind, you are ready for the spiritual journey that encompasses the remainder of this book.

Contemplation

1. The ancient Greek philosopher Empedocles said, "God is a circle whose center is everywhere and circumference is nowhere..." What comes to your mind and how do you feel when you think about this definition and description of God?
2. Think for a moment about infinity -- infinite time, infinite space. What feelings do you get when you think about these ideas? Does your inability to comprehend these concepts stop you from trying to understand them?
3. The great Seer and teacher Maharishi Mahesh Yogi said, "The thought of God finds fulfillment in its own extinction." We must transcend our thoughts, minds, and bodies to know the realm of God. During the practice of meditation, all our thoughts and sensations dissolve; and in that state of consciousness, we find ourselves in the realm of the divine. Think about your prayer and meditative experiences as letting go everything that is 'not God.'
4. After we let go all of our preconceived ideas of God, what is left -- what is your image of God? How do you personally feel about letting go of your beliefs and thoughts about God? What feelings does this activity stir up in you?
5. Search through your house to find a religious object, such as a statue or picture of Christ, or another deity or saint. Place it in front of you about 3 feet away. Gaze at it intensely. Let yourself become completely absorbed in it. Think of the qualities of infinite love, compassion, truth, etc. associated with the deity or saint. Just let your consciousness soak in these qualities. Continue this exercise for about 20 minutes, and then reflect on your experiences.

6. Over the next 24 hours, choose three individuals, and interview them about their feelings toward, experiences with, and beliefs about God. Compare and contrast their responses with your own.
7. Spend about 10 minutes thinking about your life. Think of times when you felt "unseen hands" assisting you or helping you. What was this experience like and how did you explain it to yourself? Write about these experiences in your journal.

Application

1. God Is My Breath.

   Close your eyes and practice some gentle breathing for a few minutes. Become aware of your body and your breathing. Stay with this awareness for a few minutes... Have the idea that the air entering your lungs as you inhale is infused with the power and presence of God. Think of the oxygen coming into your lungs as a vast sea that surrounds you, an endless ocean saturated with God's presence and being... Have the idea that while you are drawing air into your lungs, you are drawing in the power and presence of God... feel this each time that you breathe in. Just gently stay with this awareness... become conscious of God's Spirit coming into you, and filling your lungs and your body with divine energy ... now have the idea that, as you exhale and breathe out, you can imagine that you are breathing out all of your impurities: your fears, your stresses, your conflicts, all of your negativity. See your whole body becoming radiant, sparkling and alive, through this simple process of breathing in God's life-affirming energy, bestowing spirit and breathing out all of your impurities...

just stay with this awareness for a few minutes. And then calmly rest.

2. Not this. Not this.

   Again, close your eyes, and take a few slow breaths to develop an internal focus. Watch your thoughts. With each thought that arises in your mind, have the awareness that the thought, any thought, is not God. As God lies beyond the mental process of thinking, God is the energy that produces the thoughts, the Witness of the thoughts, but is not the discrete thoughts your mind produces. So as thoughts arise, gently remind yourself: 'This thought is not God. That thought is not God.' Be as gentle with yourself as you know how to be. When you enter a state with few or no thoughts, rest in that meditative state, and experience yourself on a deeper level. This technique, from the Indian philosophy of Vedanta, is called, 'Neti, Neti' (not this, not this).

Lesson Nine

DEALING WITH THE BODY

• • • • •

Illumination

"The body is an instrument and a servant of the soul, and not its prison..."

Swami Sivananda

One of the greatest saints of the 20th century, Swami Sivananda, 1887-1963, was a Hindu spiritual teacher and founder of the Divine Life Society. He worked as a doctor in Malaya and later published over 200 books on yoga and nearly 300 books on a wide variety of topics.

Examination

Having made a decision to embrace our spirituality, it is perhaps ironic that one of the early topics to consider is the care of our physical bodies! There are many opinions that the body is either unessential or perhaps an impediment to the pursuit of spirituality, but nothing could be further from the truth. Denying the body or harming the body in any way is likely to take your further from, not closer to, your goal.

We cannot emphasize enough the importance of care of the body, simply because it is all we really have... at least in this life, in space and time. Most people take better care of their cars and homes than they do of their physical instrument, the body! We pollute it with alcohol, drugs, and bad food, and expose it to great stress through poor sleep habits, workaholism, and other negative habits. We act as if it is infinite and can last forever. It cannot, and it does not.

If we do not like the body, we sometimes denigrate it and neglect it. Sometimes we try to over-control it through rigorous exercise and a strict diet. We love the pleasure that it gives us, and hate the pain that it causes us during illness and injury. At one time in the West, in a certain developmental period of the Judeo-Christian spiritual tradition, the body was despised by spiritual seekers—neglected and even tortured to negate its influence. Even in some eastern spiritual traditions, depriving the body and its senses of fulfillment was seen as an aid to spiritual growth and development. For example, before the Buddha found the middle path to spiritual enlightenment, he treated his body poorly, depriving it of proper nutrition and rest. Most of us feel ambivalent about our relationship with our body -- a kind of love-hate relationship. Even St. Francis of Assisi seemed to have experienced this -- in his now famous prayer for peace, he asks God to make the body and instrument of God's peace. On other occasions he referred to the body as "brother ass."

Strictly speaking, a well-cared for physical body can allow you to have a much easier time participating in spiritual activity. Moreover, if we are worried about our physical health, sitting to meditate, chant, pray, or contemplate may be easier said than done. As the mind and the body are interdependent, if the body is not healthy, the mind will be affected. Worry about the condition of the body will make it more difficult to focus the mind on a spiritual practice. A healthy body allows the mind freedom from worry in order to focus on loftier goals. If you are healthy, you can more easily train your mind to think in productive ways rather than have your mind think constantly about improving your health.

It is best to view the body as the conduit or vehicle for consciousness that we seek to expand, clarify, and amplify in our lives. Consequently, we need to take assiduous care of the body, as we need it to function at optimal levels for as long as possible. This is most obvious when we think of the nervous system, perhaps the subtlest and most intricate of the body systems. How can we even conceive of, much less experience, God or spirituality without a well-functioning central nervous system?

The central nervous system includes the autonomic system, comprised of the sympathetic and parasympathetic systems. The sympathetic nervous system is activated or engaged whenever we encounter a stressful situation. Typically, this occurs by activating the flight-or-fight-or-freeze response in which the heart beats faster, the breath becomes shallow and quicker, muscles tighten, and we begin to perspire. The sympathetic system remains engaged when we have chronic stress (financial problems, ongoing unemployment/underemployment, relationship problems, etc.). We know, from decades of research, that chronic stress leads to a chronically overactive sympathetic nervous system. When this system remains in a heightened state of alarm over an extended period, we are prone to develop higher levels of blood pressure and artery-clogging plaques, and increase our risk for a variety of physical problems, including headache and stroke. Stress slowly continues to deplete the body's energy resources until the stressful event(s) has passed and the parasympathetic nervous system has restored it to homeostasis (normal functioning). When people live in stressful conditions for months or years, substantial damage to the nervous system and other physical systems can occur.

Elevated levels of stress appear to have become part and parcel of everyday life. The 2014 Annual Stress Survey from the American Psychological Association reveals that the average stress level of Americans is 4.9 (on a 10-point scale, in which 1 = little or no stress and 10 = a great deal of stress); 29% reported their stress levels increased in the previous year, while only 18% of Americans said their stress levels decreased in the previous year. One quarter of all Americans said that stress had a strong or very strong impact on their health, most likely because they have been placing excessive demands on their sympathetic nervous systems. These individuals keep the HPA axis – the hypothalamus, pituitary gland, and adrenal glands – engaged over extended time periods. The HPA axis produces hormones that prompt the adrenal glands to release cortisol (stress hormones) throughout the body. High levels of cortisol increase appetite and lead to the buildup of fat tissue, and subsequent weight gain. Interestingly, 41% of millennials agree that they have eaten too much unhealthy food in the past month due to stress.

Currently, it does not appear that Americans manage their stress in appropriate ways. While slightly more than half of millennials report having lain awake at night in the past month due to stress, 57% of this demographic report that listening to music is their primary stress management technique. We wonder if this technique adds to the problem rather than creates a solution. In any event, the data provide testimony that, as a nation, we need to lower our stress levels and take better care of our physical bodies than we do, particularly if we aspire to attain elevated states of conscious awareness. If we hope to have expanded levels of consciousness, our nervous systems need to be in excellent condition.

Eastern philosophical traditions, particularly yoga, conceptualize the body as existing in various levels or states. A simplified version of this teaching is that the great Self animates, or enlivens, four separate bodies: gross, subtle, causal, and supracausal. The densest is the gross or physical body, with which we see, feel, and identify ourselves as objective beings. The gross body grows old, experiences pain, and dies. We are cautioned by the great spiritual traditions not to overidentify with the gross body. This is conceived as bondage or ignorance because the gross body is impermanent and is not our true identity. There is a delicate balancing act here. As St. Theresa of Avila warns us, we should not overly pamper the body, or focus too much on its adornment -- this promotes overidentification and is a waste of energy. Nor is it beneficial to seek simply to satisfy its constant yearnings for sensual pleasures.

The subtle body, also known as the astral body, is a less dense, nonphysical body. It resides within (so to speak) and interpenetrates the gross physical body. The subtle body houses our emotions, and is the body in which we dream at night. Moreover, all of our karmic impressions – the residuals of actions taken in this lifetime and other lifetimes – reside within the subtle body. The third body, the causal, is active in deep sleep and in profound meditation. The causal body resides in the heart. The fourth body, the highest, is the Supracasual. It is the seat of the Supreme Self and resides in the crown of the head, at the highest energy center of the body (the Sahasrara chakra). When our awareness is permanently established in this energy center, we perceive only Unity-Awareness (see *The Sacred Power* by Swami Kripananda).

According to the Hindu Scriptures called the Upanishads, for optimal physical functioning, we need a balance in our diet, physical exercise, routine, and rest. Diet is extremely important. If we overeat or eat the wrong foods, our digestion is affected, and we will not have the energy needed for meditation or other spiritual practices. In fact, the science of Ayurveda, the traditional system of Indian medicine, prescribes different diets depending upon your 'type' (Vata, Pitta, or Kapha). It is important to eat food appropriate for your type as well as food in season and food that is 'alive' with energy. Farm fresh foods or natural foods picked from your garden are foods that are 'alive' with energy, compared with processed foods, stale foods, or many canned and frozen foods. The digestive fire, called Agni in Ayurveda, must be kept strong and burn high, in order to make the most of our meditation sessions. Meditation on an empty stomach is preferable. We cannot meditate on full stomachs or after having eaten heavy foods, too many fried foods, or foods that do not contain enough of the 'life force' (as contained in organic or farm fresh foods). Herbal and other supplements, while consistent with a yogic lifestyle, may not be necessary for persons with a healthy diet of fresh foods.

Physical exercise is extremely important, as it keeps the body and mind energized, supple, and alert. Hatha yoga, which includes stretching, physical postures called Asanas, and other movement activities (walking, swimming, Tai Chi) are also excellent supports for many spiritual practices. Massages, particularly Ayurvedic massages, are quite beneficial. One of the reasons physical exercise, stretching, and hatha yoga are important is because it allows the meditator to sit comfortably for a long period of time with a straight back or spine, rather than slouching. Posture is a vital component in meditation, chanting, and prayer. When we first began to sit for meditation, it was painful to sit cross-legged for very long. To this very day, it is amazing how much our posture continues to improve, not just when sitting for meditation, but at other times as well!

Deep, lasting, and sufficient rest also is a recommended practice to rejuvenate the body. It is important to discriminate, and not push the body to do too much when in craves rest. In general, it is helpful to go to bed before 10:00 p.m., and rise at about 6:00 a.m. and meditate.

Like many other things in life, a daily routine is considered very important in pursuing spirituality. Engaging in the same practices and habits on a daily schedule brings the best results.

Swami Sivananda makes the important point that the purpose of the body is to serve the soul, not the other way around. The body, like the mind, is a tool, and these tools serve us not only on a physical level, but also serve our higher bodies on astral, causal, and supercausal levels. When we identify with our physical bodies, and then make disparaging remarks about how our body looks, we are stuck in the level of physicality, rather than nourishing our soul or experiencing higher levels of Being.

It is essential that if we are to experience love as a constant in our lives – love for others, love for nature, love for animals, birds, fish, etc. – we need to start with love for ourselves and this includes love for our bodies. If we find that we have intense requirements to feel love for our bodies ("I will love my body as soon as I lose xx lbs. and fit into a size xx.") we are caught in the type of attachment that will keep us limited to serving our egos. Thus it is essential to feel love, starting NOW, for your body as it is. There are several methods to achieve this love.

Start by loving your body for what it is and what it does, rather than how it appears (especially to others). Love it because through your body, you can use your senses and see, hear, taste, feel, and touch the world in which you live. Next, love your body because you can move from one place to another in it. Experience the joy of movement when you walk or jog. Experience the joy of breathing contentedly as you sit. Love that your hands can be used to manipulate objects, such as pens, pencils, and cooking utensils. Love that you can have physical pleasure in your body. More than these, love that your body is your friend, and exists so that you may grow and evolve on all levels, particularly psychological and spiritual levels.

Contemplation

1. A great Indian saint said that we should treat the body like a guest or visitor -- it has come but must go, eventually. How does that make you feel? Does it sit well with you? How do you feel when your guests leave? Can you imagine that is the way you will feel when you die? Have you ever had an out-of-body experience? Can you imagine yourself without a body or what Zen Buddhists call our original face?

2. Do you take better care of your car than your body? Why?!
3. In most Eastern spiritual traditions, the direct relationship between body and mind is emphasized. Therefore, taking care of the body improves the functioning of the mind. Have you found this to be true in your own life? Exercise is often recommended to reduce the probability of developing Alzheimer's disease (senile dementia). Can you imagine why?

Application

1. Go to bed tonight at 10:00 p.m. and sleep until 6 a.m. Rise and meditate for 20 minutes. After your meditation period, record in your journal how you feel. Do you have more alertness? More calm? Greater energy? Compare how you feel to other days in which you went to sleep much later.
2. Watch what you eat for the next 24 hours -- what does this say about you? How can you improve upon your diet?
3. Write down a plan for balance for your body that you can commit to and carry out for the next 90 days.
4. Try something new, like taking a 30-minute nap late in the afternoon before supper. Notice how it makes you feel. Try something else new, such as walking, making a positive change in your diet, or getting a massage. Notice how differently you feel. According to Ayurvedic medicine, afternoon naps need to be completed by 3:00 p.m., so as not to interfere with your sleep in the evening. If you take a nap, do you feel better if you finish by 3:00 p.m.?
5. Make a list of ways in which you appreciate your body, including ways you appreciate internal organs such as your heart, kidneys, and lungs. Talk to your body and give it thanks

for all it does to serve you and your Soul. Notice how you feel after 30 – 60 seconds of expressing your love and appreciation for your body.

6. Spend a few minutes relaxing, and then spend ten minutes performing mantra meditation (coordinate a sound or word, such as 'calm' and 'relax,' with the incoming and outgoing breaths). Following this meditation period, allow yourself to visualize a soft blue healing light over each part of your body. Start with your head, and let it slowly descend to your neck, torso, arms, stomach, hips, thighs, lower legs, ankles, and feet. Feel its glowing warmth, its sparkle, its purity, its consciousness. Allow your attention to then focus on your breathing. As you breathe in, feel the vital energy, or prana, enter into your body. As you breathe out, feel all of your impurities and distortions leaving your body. Let this beautiful healing process go on for approximately 15 minutes, and then return to activity after a minute or two of rest.

Lesson Ten

MEDITATION

• • • • •

Illumination

"The mind turned outward results in thoughts and objects. Turned inward, it becomes its self, the Self (of all) ..."

Ramana Maharishi

Ramana Maharishi, 1879 – 1950, was an Indian sage and an Enlightened Master (Jivanmukti) by the age of 16 years. He was worshipped by thousands, and insisted that silence was the purest teaching. He recommended self-inquiry as the principle way to realize the Self.

Examination

In addition to wanting Self-knowledge, how often do you crave some genuine rest? Most of us have our minds turned outward – toward a multitude of sensory objects and tasks – all day long. And by the end of the day, we are exhausted! We try so hard to complete our daily tasks, improve ourselves, and upgrade our status with a nicer home, bigger car, or better education. There is no question that the reason we try so hard to accomplish so much is that we are searching for happiness.

Who in this world is not searching for happiness? All of the Great Beings encourage and remind us constantly that we can find happiness, but we need to search for it within ourselves, not on the outside. Maharishi Mahesh Yogi spread his Transcendental Meditation ™ all across the Americas, as well as in the East. Many of us recall The Beatles learning TM from Maharishi, and then becoming strong advocates of meditation as a spiritual discipline. As time went on, TM gained thousands upon thousands of practitioners and was discussed in the Wall Street Journal.

Meditation is a much misunderstood process. In the West we are not accustomed to taking time out during the day to engage in the practice of meditation -- it's foreign to us. When we think of meditation, mostly we think of a contemplative practice, such as pondering a spiritual question or digesting a passage from a great book, such as the Bible. In this view, meditation seems to be a mental effort that leads to a product. Or we think that meditating is doing nothing, which is generally a waste of time, and at odds with a "can do" attitude. Perhaps we have been told that if we spend time doing nothing we will become lazy, lack motivation, and lose our competitive edge.

Numerous people have become frustrated in their attempts to meditate. Many report that they could not "make my mind go blank" and simply gave up the effort. Yet many people have learned to meditate haphazardly, rather than learn from a reliable source or personal teacher. Although to this day, there are those who are reluctant to learn meditation, it is important to state that meditation is not something that is mystical or peculiar. It certainly is not a passive process in which "nothing" is happening. It can be viewed as a technique or method to help us settle down, and contact the peace and tranquility which lies within all of us. It is actually a very simple, straightforward process.

Meditation is the most natural process. It is not difficult or complicated. In general, meditation begins by shifting our attention from the external world to our own internal world. As we shift from the exterior to the interior, we experience a type of disengagement from our day-to-day mental and physical functioning. We become calm, and become absorbed in our own inner stillness. And, as we go deeper within, we begin to experience our true Self -- the Self beyond our ego, beyond our thoughts, beyond our emotions, beyond our physical sensations -- what has classically been referred to as **Pure Consciousness.** In this pure, tranquil state, we gain clarity, just as we do when the dirt and sediment in a pond clear and we can see the bottom. In this process, meditation removes the stressors that are obstacles limiting our access to inner perception and inspiration. And as these obstacles are dissolved, we gain deep rest, we gain a deep sense of recreation – re-Creation -- we let go of our old stressors and emerge, functioning from a new pattern.

When I meditate, I (Vincent) experience the most restful and energizing of states. Afterward, I am so refreshed; I have energy to spare, even though I may have been exhausted prior to a meditation session. As a psychologist, I am often asked how I can sit and listen to people's problems all day long, day after day. Quite frankly, if I did not have a regular meditation practice, I do not think I could. I certainly would not be as attentive and present with my clients. Often I find myself in a meditative state when I am sitting with clients. Rather than being unfocused or daydreaming, my focus on my clients is strong and one-pointed. It is as if only the client exists in the moment; there are few distracting thoughts regarding anyone or anything else. I am still and nonjudgmental. I sometimes feel blissful at these times. I am also aware of wanting the clients to experience the same joy from focused attention that I feel. I know that I am a good resource to them in this state.

As we practice meditation, over time we start to live our lives from the quiet core of our inner being; we cease to become easily upset over everyday matters that are trivial and inconsequential. We gain confidence, equanimity, and detachment from things which truly do not count. Pointless gossip that seems to greatly interest others starts to fade in importance. Over a long period of practice, our sense of being an individual person gently melts away, and our sense of being universal, unbounded, and connected with all things gradually takes over. As this process unfolds, deeply-rooted stress, held by the nervous system, is gently dissolved. We gain an unshakable sense of silence in the experience of an unchanging field of awareness -- we find the changeless within the constantly changing phenomenal universe, and when we do, we experience everyone as a pure, loving being!! Most importantly, we do not have to utilize effort to do this: meditation is a process of **non-doing,** rather than doing. Meditation works because it is guided by the ultimate desire in life -- the desire to discover our Inner Self.

The great Indian philosopher Krishnamurti said that meditation is not a means to an end but, rather, meditation is both the means and the end. In a sense, meditation is not simply a technique that leads us to a particular state of illumination, or peace -- it is, in itself, that state of illumination, or peace. In a way, while we meditate, we are not pursuing a path to enlightenment – we step directly into deeper levels of our own being. There are many forms of meditation, but they all assist the mind to transcend the ego and come to rest in our true **Self.**

Research on meditation shows that it reduces anxiety, depression, and other negative mood states, even as it cleanses the body, reduces blood pressure, and brings about healing in all the body systems. One of the greatest benefits of meditation is the purification of the mind. As Ram Dass has said, we are all prisoners of our own minds. Meditation gently cleans out both conscious and unconscious material that blocks our Self-Realization. Meditation leads to a great surge of energy, as it releases all of the tension we have been using to defend ourselves and hold ourselves together.

There are a few 'tips' in learning meditation that we believe will be of value to you. First, we recommend that you meditate every day, preferably 15 to 20 minutes first thing in the morning; and again, if possible, before dinner in the evening. Try to meditate at the same time each day, but, if you are not able to do so, then any time of day is good.

If you can meditate in a place that is neat and clean, you will build up a storehouse of energy in that location. Do try to simplify the environment where you meditate: make it clutter-free. If you are able to wear the same clothes each day (you can purchase white clothes for meditation from a number of websites online), the clothes will also hold your meditative energy. A quiet place will help you go deeper within your being. If you like, you can practice some hatha yoga exercises (physical postures) to invigorate the body and mind for meditation. Or you can spend 5-10 minutes chanting before you meditate. You can chant the sacred syllable 'OM,' or anything else that brings you in touch with your own inner Divinity.

It would be of great benefit if you could try to refrain from the universal tendency to judge and rate your meditation experience. ("That was a great meditation!" or "I just couldn't begin to get into it.") Approaching meditation with an attitude of curiosity, experimentation, and a desire to explore the depths of your own being will provide you with the best incentive to continue on your journey. In truth, any one meditation experience is not better or worse than any other. Just sitting down to make the effort to meditate is all you need to do.

For beginners who would like to learn more about meditation and a variety of meditation techniques, I recommend the book *Why Meditate?* by Dr. Matthieu Ricard, a student of Kangyur Rinpoche and Dilgo Khyentse Rinpoche. Written from a Buddhist perspective, this book contains many meditative practices for students of all levels. One does not have to be Buddhist, or even interested in Buddhism, to benefit from the enormous wisdom and engaging practices contained in this volume. Dr. Ricard points out that, by developing our own positive qualities through meditation, we can truly be of service to others.

A second excellent book to read in learning the fundamentals of meditation is *How to Meditate* by Pema Chodron, a Buddhist teacher and adept. She describes the many benefits that accrue to the meditator, including the development of an attitude of loving kindness toward oneself (called 'Unconditional Friendliness'). She teaches an open-eyed form of meditation that allows the student to develop an attitude of acceptance and peacefulness with all that is occurring in the present moment, but she also illustrates numerous other methods of meditation to sights and sounds.

A more advanced book on meditation is called 'Meditation for the Love of It' written by Sally Kempton, a former Vedic teaching monk, who has written extensively on the joy and benefits of engaging in a regular meditation practice. She writes from a Hindu perspective, describing how one might progress through different stages of meditation experiences.

Scientific studies demonstrate that those who meditate regularly have been able to change the structure and functioning of their brains. For example, long-time meditators have been shown to develop the parts of the brain associated with compassion toward others. Dr. Ricard noted that Mindfulness-Based Stress Reduction (MBSR), practiced for 30 minutes per day, significantly strengthened the immune system, reinforced positive emotions and the faculty of attention, reduced arterial pressure in those suffering from high blood pressure, and accelerated the healing of psoriasis. Research also suggests even a brief meditation practice affects the physical structure of the brain for the better!

Sara Lazar (2011) investigated changes in brain gray matter density in 16 persons, ages 25 – 55 years, who participated in a Mindfulness-Based Stress Reduction (MBSR) program over a period of 8 weeks, using magnetic resonance imaging to scan the brains of the participants two weeks prior and two weeks after participation in the program. Over 8 weeks, participants reported spending an average of about 27 minutes per day in meditative homework exercises. The results showed that the participants demonstrated significant increases in gray matter concentration in the hippocampus, an area of the brain associated with learning and memory. Additional improvements were identified in other brain areas, such as the posterior cingulate cortex, tempero-parietal junction, and the cerebellum.

The authors consistently find that practicing meditation in the morning changes the course of our entire day for the better. We are fresher and more self-confident. We are better able to focus on others and assist them with their problems. We more easily withstand disappointment and things not working out according to plan.

Contemplation

1. The practice of meditation is an undoing, an unraveling, a deprogramming, a deconstruction. Imagine what you would be like totally free of any and all conditioning. Imagine having no personal identity. Does this provoke any fears?
2. Most people who start meditation are perplexed and give up because they cannot control their minds. Remember, when you meditate, avoid having any expectations. Just take things gently as they come, play things as they roll, don't fight anything, and above all don't *try*. Simply be a witness to what is happening in the field of your awareness.
3. Remember that meditation is a means of purification. There may be some discomfort during meditation as we "undo" past

damage. This is normal. Simply make an effort to tolerate and watch unpleasant thoughts and feelings. You can remember, as you are dissolving deep stresses, that meditation displaces and discards them in a most natural and effortless way.

Application

1. Over the next 24 hours, meditate for two 20-minute sessions, and journal your experiences.
2. Go online and read one scientific study on the effects of meditation. Share your newfound knowledge with a friend. Check out www.TM.org, or the www.brainresearchinstitute.org.
3. Talk with friends who have been meditating for some time. Ask them why they do it and how they have benefitted from their practice.
4. Many monks and spiritual students rise between 3:00 – 6:00 a.m. to meditate. Try one meditation session prior to 6:00 am. Is your experience any different than later in the day?
5. A common Kabbalistic meditation (Kabbalah is a form of Jewish mysticism) is candle gazing. In a dark room, place a lit candle on a table. Softly gaze at it, and let it fill your mind. Become aware of its heat and energy. Notice any variations in color in the flame. Now let your awareness settle on the contrasting darkness in the room. According to some Jewish mystical texts, you may begin to see a sky blue field in the darkness in the room. This darkness is said to represent divine energy. If you do, just be a silent witness to it.
6. For those who are convinced they cannot meditate, try the following exercise. Sit straight with your eyes open. Try

facing a blank wall to minimize possible visual distractions. Place a small lit candle on a table in front of the wall and gaze at the flame. Begin to pay attention to your breathing. Employing belly breathing, or diaphramtic breathing, can be invaluable in this exercise. Play soft classical music as you try to meditate, if this exercise is difficult.

LESSON ELEVEN

ON DOUBT

• • • • •

ILLUMINATION

"Doubt is the vestibule through which all must pass before they can enter the temple of wisdom..."

Charles C. Colton

Colton, 1780-1832, was an 18th/19th century English cleric and writer who wrote the book *Many Things in Few Words*, which was highly read and praised.

EXAMINATION

Once you have achieved a reasonably healthy body and have developed a daily routine which includes meditation, there are other obstacles with which anyone on a spiritual path must contend. Primary among them are doubt and its subsequent anxiety. The opportunities for doubt are limitless, and occur whether you have been practicing spiritual disciplines for 35 days or 35 years. Each of us has considered discontinuing our practices on numerous occasions when we doubted if we were making genuine progress on the spiritual path. Doubt can give way to an experience sometimes referred to as the 'Dark Night of the Soul.' This is a term coined by St. John of the Cross, which means everything seems meaningless, pointless, futile, and worthless. Truth be told, everyone goes through periods, sometimes quite lengthy, when the practices feel empty, dry, unrewarding, and simply not worth the effort we are spending. We have asked ourselves why we are doing what we are doing, and whether we would not be better off investing our time and money into hobbies or Caribbean vacations. These periods of doubt are very unpleasant and unnerving, to say the very least.

Uncontrolled doubt can lead to uncertainty, indecision, and fear. Doubt can infect and spoil everything we consider. Chronic obsessive doubt leads to weariness and mental fatigue. It can sap our strength and vitality. When we experience doubt, we feel stuck. We feel pulled in different directions. We can become immobilized. Such immobilization is at odds with growth and development. We need to continually evolve on the spiritual path, and doubt is one of the great obstacles to evolution.

In the 21st century, it has become fashionable and a mark of intelligence to doubt authority. We believe we are exercising our intelligence by doubting what we are told, and are quick to dismiss wisdom, no matter what the basis for it may be. After all, we don't want to be pushovers. As a result, teachers, doctors, scholars, and spiritual adepts are more likely to be doubted than believed. In colleges and universities, critical analysis is taught and valued, but, when taken to extreme, our brightest students come to doubt all sources of knowledge. Masters and teachers from ancient times are easily dismissed or not considered at all, as if the sum total of human knowledge has been developed over the past 50 years, or since the advent of the computer and the Internet.

In contrast, we find, in our clinical psychology practices, the most highly anxious patients typically believe most of what they think, without any critical analysis whatsoever. They believe that something is true simply because they thought it. Thus, when it comes to doubt, there are two contrasting tendencies. The first is to quickly doubt and reject information without carefully considering it; the second is to accept an idea without any type of examination or scrutiny. Both tendencies are flawed, as it is important to thoroughly understand, test, and examine a spiritual principle before adopting it.

The type of doubt to which we refer in this lesson is not a simple matter of doubting a fact, such as who won the World Series in a particular year; rather, we are concerned with doubting the direction or course we want to pursue in life. When we doubt our spiritual teachers, teachings, practices, and progress, we are saying that perhaps they are not worthwhile or effective. Or we believe that the teachers and practices are fine, but that we ourselves are deficient when trying to implement them. That is, we believe that the practices have worked for others, but they will not work for us. We just don't think that our efforts will lead to a positive outcome. Life can appear meaningless at this time, as if nothing we try to do will lead to spiritual benefit and upliftment.

Yet doubt is likely a prerequisite for the development of true wisdom, as Charles Colton informs us. It is a necessary part of the spiritual journey. If this is true, what shall we do about doubt? We can obtain some ideas from the spiritual masters who have gone before us. The great First Nation Peoples sage, Ponca Chief White Eagle said, "When you are in doubt, be still and wait; when doubt no longer exists for you, then go forward with courage. So long as the mists envelop you be still; be still until the sunlight pours through and dispels the mists – as it surely will. Then act with courage." The stillness can be achieved through patience, deep meditation, and contemplation.

A doubting mind is an agitated, distracted, and anxious mind. We need to tolerate the doubt and subsequent agitation without trying to eliminate it as soon as possible. Perhaps the doubt will compel us to learn something about ourselves that had previously been hidden from conscious awareness. Or the doubt may help us strive to seek assistance from others. As we become still and contemplate the doubt, sooner or later a resolution arises from the depths of our being, from Inner Awareness. We can then leap into action. Chief White Eagle tells us that when we are enveloped in the mist, the sunlight will surely pour through us to dispel it.

The great Indian sage Ramana Maharishi said that doubt arises because of the absence of surrender. Surrender of what? As the first step of Alcoholics Anonymous recommends, it is surrender of the ego – the sense of "I-ness" - and its control. We let go of the ego and embrace the Higher Self, our inner core of illuminating consciousness. When we transcend reliance upon the ego and the intellect as our sources of knowledge and wellbeing and embrace our true nature, doubt is automatically resolved. As our consciousness comes to rest in pure awareness, we become more and more stable in our day-to-day practice, and doubt begins to wither away, because it is not supported by pure consciousness. None other than Jesus the Christ, the pinnacle of human spiritual evolution, lost faith, and fell into a state of doubt. This was the beginning of his passion. His anguish was lifted and his resolve regained when he let go and allowed God's will and divine intelligence to flood into his consciousness. Through surrender, his doubts ceased to limit the strength he needed to fulfill his destiny.

Maharishi Mahesh Yogi, the founder of Transcendental Meditation, suggests we can counter our doubt with... more doubt! In other words, why not doubt our doubt? On a mundane level, we ask ourselves why we would think that our doubt could possibly be the correct form of action. For example, suppose we doubt that we can ever succeed in, or benefit from, meditation. We are sure we are correct, because we tried in the past and could not get into a meditative state. Pursuing Maharishi's suggestion, we might say to ourselves, "Am I 100% certain that, because I did not succeed in the past, I cannot succeed now? How do I know this to be true?" Perhaps we are making great progress in our spiritual practices, but simply don't recognize the signs. We may have received great teachings, and our doubts can simply represent last ditch efforts of the ego to remain in control.

Learning to doubt one's doubt is a principle from his science of creative intelligence and a principal reason why the mechanics of Transcendental Meditation work so well. With Transcendental Meditation, the thinking process, which normally occupies most of our awareness, is transcended through utilization of the thinking process itself. In that technique, a mantra or sound is utilized to refine thought, until it becomes so refined it no longer exists. What is left is pure awareness, and the brightness of inner knowledge. And this is a state of awareness free from doubt and other mental distortions. This is our natural state, before the arising of doubtful thoughts.

It appears that doubt almost always surfaces as we expand our consciousness and open our awareness; and, as Charles Colton suggests, doubt is virtually a necessary experience for those who seek wisdom. Remaining on the spiritual path requires perseverance, courage, and forbearance. Doubts almost always arise like weeds in the garden of these virtues. Consider the great Indian epic, The Mahabharata, which is a story about a great war for domination of the earth that took place 1000 or more years BCE. Arjuna, the protagonist in this spiritual masterpiece, is the greatest archer of his day, a fearless warrior who struck terror in the hearts of his enemies on the battlefield. Yet when he was faced with perhaps the greatest battle of his life, a battle against his own kinsmen, he faltered. He was required to fight against, required to potentially kill, his esteemed teachers, friends, and relatives. His courage turned to terror. His normally balanced and steady mind swirled with confusion. His strong body slumped in his chariot as he fell to the floor. Doubt had taken over his entire mind. He was a man in great conflict. As a brave and steel warrior, he was obliged to subdue his enemies. Yet this time his enemies were blood relatives whom he loved. How could he justify fighting those he loved, some of whom were his mentors and taught him much of what he knew? He was paralyzed with fear and he became incapacitated. If doubt can do this to one of the bravest individuals depicted in ancient literature, what chance do we have?! Fortunately for Arjuna, his charioteer and guide was Lord Krishna. Krishna was a god who would bestow divine wisdom on Arjuna. Slowly, patiently, and persistently, he drew Arjuna out of his doubt-plagued state of consciousness and purified his awareness. He helped Arjuna gain clarity and resolve.

When we are in a state of doubt, we can't see reality, and we become overcome by distortions in our awareness. Krishna, in this tale, represents pure consciousness, the divine wisdom that lies latent in all of us. This pure knowledge that lies at the core of our being can dissolve our doubts and allow us to go forward in our evolution. Arjuna was paralyzed to act, but when he gained clarity, he leapt into action. He was a warrior. This was his Dharma. Dharma is one's purpose in life. As a warrior, his Dharma was to fight, and fight he did, winning the battle of the day and vanquishing his foes.

You will, unquestionably, struggle with doubt in your life. You may doubt your decisions, the love of your spouse, your capacity to deal with adversity, your competencies, or even your very sense of who you are. As inevitable as doubt is, just as important is its resolution. When I (Vincent) have doubted whether I am truly progressing in my spiritual practices, my 'Sadhana,' I ask myself if I am a different person now than I was before I began to practice. I ask how I would like my life to go forward. What do I want to accomplish in life? What type of person do I want to be? What personal qualities do I want to achieve? Who do I want to emulate during the remainder of my life? In other words, I try to take an inventory of myself: values, goals, and strategies. When I have rededicated my life to my spiritual path, I have typically moved forward in my capacities for self-reflection, patience, tolerance, generosity, and loving-kindness. My experience is that most doubts have eventually resolved, and I have found my way to a deeper level of peace and joy in my spiritual practice.

Contemplation

1. As the quote by Charles Colton implies, doubt is paradoxical—even necessary—for the birth of truth. Descartes said, "If you would be a real seeker of the truth, it is necessary, at least once in your life, to doubt, as far as possible, all things." This is obviously a very powerful statement. Think of times in your life when you were seized by great doubt. How was it resolved? What positive developments rose out of your doubt? Can you see how doubting everything to the fullest extent can be the basis for spiritual growth?
2. Albert Einstein said that the most important aspect in life is to not stop questioning. What is the relationship between challenging mental inquiry - and its implied doubt - with spiritual evolution?
3. We all have doubts -- about God, truth, religion, the goodness of man, and the recovery process, for example. What would you consider the biggest doubt of your life? How have you coped with it? What have you done to resolve it thus far in your life?

Application

1. On a piece of paper, write down all the certainties of your life. Next, write down all the things in life that you most doubt. Looking at your lists, what are the differences and what are the similarities between them?
2. Have you developed a habit of doubting your words, your ideas, and decisions? Try recognizing your doubting habit, if you have one, and try to move forward without doubts. If you have made a poor choice, you can simply change it and

make a better one. It is better to develop the habit of trust and confidence in yourself than to chronically doubt yourself.

3. Sometimes we feel paralyzed by doubt and stand still for a long period of time as we are fearful of taking the wrong course of action. Over the next 24 hours, perform one action that will help resolve one of your doubts.
4. Identify the one aspect of your life you doubt most. After breathing quietly for a few minutes, mentally recite the doubt in a concise manner: in one sentence. Then give the doubt to God, and ask that God deal with the doubt and manage it. Imagine that this doubt now belongs to God, not to you. Sit quietly for at least 5 minutes. Be aware over the next week to see if there are any ways in which God has sent you information that you can use to resolve the doubt.

LESSON TWELVE

DEALING WITH PROBLEMS

• • • • •

ILLUMINATION

"Problems are messages."

Shakti Gawain

Gawain (b. 1948) is a New Age and personal development author, a best-seller for over 25 years. Her books have sold over 10 million copies.

"I tell them there's no problems, only solutions."

John Lennon

Lennon, 1940-1980, was a songwriter and singer who was a founding member of 'The Beatles' rock and roll group. As a peace activist he was known for criticizing American involvement in the Vietnam war. Lennon was a long-time meditator.

Examination

Once I (Vincent) began to embrace a spiritual path, I knew I would be on it for the rest of my life. I had no doubts about my teacher being the perfect one to guide me. After I became a regular meditator, I studied the teachings of my tradition, and surrendered many of my doubts. I hoped that, as a result of my spiritual dedication and practice, most of my problems would be behind me, even though I was warned that this wouldn't happen. Well, those who warned me were right! While some of my problems were behind me, a lot were ahead of me! (And there is quite a long way to go yet in this lifetime, I suspect). When I encounter problems, it is tempting for me to think that I have not learned anything on the spiritual path, and shouldn't even count myself as a spiritual person. Of course, this is simply my ego talking, as if being a 'spiritual person' confers some special status, or gives one a free pass in life when it comes to not having to undergo personal problems. (Hint: 'It doesn't.')

Embracing a spiritual path is not the end of worldly problems, and in some ways may create new ones! For one thing, it is easy to be on the 'ego trip' of being a spiritual person, as if we have gained membership to a new, exclusive club. It is also tempting to believe that the existence of personal problems may mean that we are not making any progress on our spiritual path, or that we are engaging with our path insufficiently or inadequately. Evidence from individuals who have become spiritual Masters suggests that they confronted significant problems immediately prior to attaining Self-Realization. Eckhart Tolle, in the introduction to his book *The Power of Now*, describes facing depression and suicidal thoughts prior to his spiritual awakening. Jan

Frazier worried constantly about the possibility of developing breast cancer before she, too, had an awakening. Everyone has obstacles to Self-Realization and Enlightenment, but all the Masters agree on one thing -- problems are opportunities in disguise, opportunities to awaken us. It has been said that, as we journey forward on a spiritual path, sometimes the problems become more, not less, intense.

Pema Chodren, the wonderful Buddhist teacher, advises us to embrace our problems, because they will be the vehicles to transport us to higher states of consciousness. Problems in life are the stimuli to help us transcend: they can be used for a higher purpose. The great psychologist and philosopher William James said that struggles excite us and inspire us. Imagine a life with no problems or obstacles. What would there be to do? What would motivate us? Having problems is not a great obstacle in life if we learn how we deal with them. Problems are to be transcended. As a general guideline, we do what we can to surmount them, and then we give them over to God.

We have no intention to minimize the very real pain of emotional, physical, financial, work, housing, and interpersonal problems. The existence of difficulties in life is all too obvious. Sometimes there are real and substantial problems about which we cannot help but complain. Thus we are not recommending that we should not grieve our losses when confronted with problems. And we most certainly appreciate the value in commiserating with others who are struggling in life.

How we perceive problems and react to them is the real key. The best course is to interpret every problem as an opportunity to strengthen our relationship with and trust in our Inner Divinity, or Source. We can recognize problems as gateways to gain strength, knowledge, and courage. Jesus suffered tremendously. So did the Buddha. Their reactions to problems led to an eternal awakening, and the possibility for salvation and enlightenment for all of humankind for all eternity. We need to treat problems in the same way that these great Masters did, and we, too, have the possibility of bringing about great transformations in ourselves and others. The Chinese classic, the 'I Ching' (Book of Changes), characterizes problems much like rocks in a river -- the river doesn't get upset or complain about the rocks in its path. Rather, it simply flows around them, over them, or under them, in an effortless fashion. We, too, can be like the river. Do not make too much out of problems: ignore them if you can. Don't let them stop you. It is not necessary to criticize yourself or negatively judge yourself for having problems. Your problems are your tickets to personal growth. Allow your own energy and vitality to propel you onward, despite obstacles in your path. Zen clearly states that problems help a man advance in life -- a man without problems gets lazy and judgmental. He loses incentive to evolve. Zen also tells us to develop equanimity in the face of problems.

Zen tells us to be impervious to problems. When you encounter a problem, learn what you are doing wrong, learn what you need to change. A problem may be telling us that we are not living in accord with nature -- that we are out of balance, and it's time to get back in balance. For example, perhaps we are eating too much or too little, or the wrong type of food at the wrong time. Look for the teaching moment when you encounter a problem. What potential strengths and abilities within you can be utilized to meet the problem? What resources do you have that you have never used until now? Meeting a problem may bring out your latent strengths and skills. Dealing with problems cultivates our character and draws out qualities we might never have realized we had, had we not confronted a problem. When you contemplate a problematic situation and cannot identify anything you need to change, then perhaps the best course of action is to simply wait and see if the problem disappears on its own.

One course of action that certainly will not help is excessive worry. Obsessive thinking about or preoccupation with problems will not lead to solutions, although we may naively believe that if we are worrying about our problems, at least we are doing something to try to solve them. We most certainly are not! In fact, excessive worry only serves to increase our stress levels and tax our sympathetic nervous system, as discussed in the preceding chapter. Time is better used in problem-solving or thinking of various solutions, rather than repeated worry.

And remember this: all human beings **are** problems... we are incomplete, we are imperfect, fragmented, and striving for wholeness. Our minds and our egos are the cradle of our problems and they must be transcended. The voluminous amount of research on Transcendental Meditation, for example, shows that a whole spectrum of problems can be erased by the simple process of transcendence. That was my (David's) experience; my panic attacks led to enlightenment led me to more enlightened functioning. Arjuna's dilemma on the battlefield, in the great epic the Bhagavad-Gita, led to his own enlightenment, and victory over delusion. Christ's passion saved the human race. Gautama Buddha's struggle led to his emancipation, and the possibility of emancipation for all. Remember the old saying: necessity is the mother of invention. Joyfully and gallantly confronting our problems pushes us to a new, deeper level of partnership with our spirit.

People often wonder how they can tell if they are making progress in their spiritual pursuits. Are there any guideposts? Yes, there are many. One guidepost is that when we have a problem, we are not too defensive to consider what our role in creating the problem might have been and to change our behavior if it needs to be adjusted. We do not become so paralyzed by anxiety and guilt that we are afraid to engage in critical self-examination and analysis. Furthermore, once we alter our behavior, we can easily let go of negative self-judgment about our behavior. We can allow past negative behaviors to recede into the past, without continuing to berate ourselves for them. As we continue to travel on a spiritual path and continue to encounter problems, we more easily let go of them, or attempt a solution without fear and judgment.

Still another guidepost is that we begin to reduce our expectations for others; most importantly, our expectations for how things "should be." We more comfortably accept things as they are and, as a result, fewer problems seem to exist. Rather than insisting things be "right" or "wrong," we seek to understand and feel compassion for others.

Contemplation

1. Have you experienced problems that seemed to disappear, or at least diminish, over time? The next time you encounter an obstacle or a problem, see if it is possible to avoid fighting it. Try to sidestep it, rather than become fatigued confronting it. This is the advice of Maharishi Mahesh Yogi.
2. List the top five problems in your life and define them. What do they all have in common? Do you see any trends? Do you

consider them solvable or insolvable? If they were solved or removed, how would your life be different?

3. Imagine a life with absolutely no problems whatsoever -- what do you think it would be like? What would you do with your time?
4. How do people you admire deal with problems? Think of a big problem from the past -- what worked in overcoming it? What did not work? What did this problem teach you and how did it change you?

Application

1. Take a walk in nature, in a meadow, by a stream, or through the woods. Observe the animals, plants, and trees. How do they face adversity, such as temperature changes, diseases, attacks by predators, etc.? Do they worry, do they fret, do they work hard?
2. Let's pretend that you have absolutely no problems in your life for the next 24 hours. After you go through your life for the next day, write down your experiences, and share them with someone.
3. Think about and write down an analysis of your character and personality. How have life's problems and challenges shaped your personality and character? What was the greatest problem you have faced in the past and overcome? What has been the cumulative effect of all your problems, and how you dealt with them? Think of a problem that you did not "solve". What did that teach you about yourself in life?
4. This is a classic form of meditation. Get a picture or statue of a great saint, such as St. Francis, or great person, such as

George Washington or Mahatma Gandhi. Allow your eyes to gently focus on the picture or figurine—allow your attention to be absorbed into it. Just stay with this innocent awareness. As you become more and more absorbed, begin to think about and feel those qualities that you associate with this great saint or person. Feel those qualities bubbling up inside of you, feel those qualities entering into you, call to mind how these great individuals dealt with problems and obstacles in their lives, and visualize yourself doing the same thing in your own life. When you are finished, journal your experience.

LESSON THIRTEEN

MISTAKES AND FAILURES

• • • • •

ILLUMINATION

"If you shut your door to all errors, truth will be shut out..."

Rabindrinath Tagore

Tagore, 1861-1941, was a Bengali renaissance man who was the first non-European to win the Nobel Prize in Literature in 1913. He was a gifted poet and wrote beautiful prose and poetry in colloquial Bengali language.

"The cornerstone of the temple is not higher than the lowest stone of the foundation."

Khalil Gibran

A Lebanese-American artist, poet, and writer, Gibran, 1883-1931, wrote the classic book, The Prophet, in 1923. He is the third best-selling poet of all time.

Examination

Imagine you are in a giant maze, like a corn stalk maze at Halloween. You have never seen it before. Trying hard to get through it, you venture down path after path after path, eventually succeeding after many failed attempts. You are incredibly relieved as you finally make it through.

Proceeding in life can feel very much like this. I recall receiving my 3rd quarter grade in my 12th grade Calculus class. The teacher announced each of the students' grades aloud. When he came to my name, he paused before announcing, slowly, "Morello ... 95!" This grade was substantially better than the ones I received during the first two quarters. Admittedly I was one of the least motivated students in the class. The teacher then paused to ask me if I knew why I earned a 95. When I replied that I had no idea, he explained, "You have already made every mistake it is possible to make in Calculus. You can't possibly make any more!" I suppose I was learning Calculus the hard way and perhaps the long way, just like the individual making one mistake after the other in the corn maze; but the good news is that I was learning the subject. My numerous errors were paying off.

When problems arise, as we discussed in the previous chapter, we can deny having them, or we can admit to having them and try to work toward solving them. Trying to solve a problem always entails an element of risk. In my psychotherapy practice, I find that many people are afraid to take risks and attempt new behaviors because they are not guaranteed that things will work out perfectly. The problem is that life provides no such guarantees, and if one waits until success is assured, then he just might wait forever. As Tagore says, if we close the door to all errors, that very same closed door prevents us from seeing the Truth. The greatest inventors and entrepreneurs are those who are undaunted when things do not work out well, as they are overflowing in conviction that they can succeed. On the spiritual path, it is often necessary to risk trying new ways of understanding oneself and others, and take additional risk by changing behaviors.

Paradoxically, progress on the spiritual path is not necessarily about getting everything right. Growing up in the Catholic faith, I was presented with images of saints who epitomized virtues such as chastity, faith, and purity. I assumed, or was taught, that the saints were beings who never sinned and never made mistakes, so it was natural to believe that if I could learn never to sin or make mistakes – not that these two outcomes are exactly equivalent – then I could become saintly.

Learning about the internal states of saints from various traditions, it is apparent that becoming enlightened is not about doing everything right or perfectly; it is not about eliminating all of our mistakes. For one thing, it is not always possible to know exactly what a mistake is and what it is not. Sometimes what we think of as an error can turn out to have been a very good thing. But, more to the point, the state of sainthood, or Self-Realization, is more about being perfectly attuned to the needs of each individual moment, understanding the Truth in that situation, and responding in the perfect manner. Great Beings describe living in the Truth as being analogous to turning on the light in a dark room, not simply tidying up the room and eliminating the clutter.

The word for 'teacher' in Sanskrit - 'Guru' – consists of the two syllables Gu and Ru, which refer to darkness and light. The true teacher, the true Guru, dispels the darkness in the seekers' understanding by turning on the light, illuminating the Truth for the spiritual seeker. Thus, great teachers since the ancient Greeks have placed paramount importance on the need to discover the Truth of ourselves and of each other. Great beings certainly encourage us to eliminate sins and eliminate mistakes as important elements in our spiritual practice, but there is more on the road to enlightenment than the elimination of mistakes.

Certainly the great beings do not encourage us to try to "look good" in front of others. How often do we try to do things perfectly, so that others will have a positive image of us? In this case, our goal is actually to acquire the admiration of others as much as it is to do the right thing. Scriptures from all traditions recommend focusing on how God values us, not what our friends, neighbors, and coworkers think of us. Trying to be perfect in the eyes of others can simply be a means to puff up our egos, simultaneously increasing our sense of self-importance and self-acceptance. We would do well to evaluate why we need to be more acceptable to others, and whether it is worth trying to look error-free for others in the first place. Fr. Thomas Merton said, "The logic of worldly success rests on the fallacy, the strange error, that our perfection depends on the thoughts and opinions and applause of other men..."

Mistakes and failures are inevitable in any pursuit, and the same is true when traversing the spiritual path. Failures can be reframed or conceptualized as 'The Road to Success.' That is, mistakes and failures are considered a necessary component of the learning process. Every time we make a mistake, we can evaluate our behavior, adjust our thinking, and utilize this feedback for the next occasion. That is why we prefer to regard failures and mistakes as signs of developing success: an apparent failure now has, embedded within it, a future success. In a way, then, there may be just as much truth to be learned in a failure as in a success, if we can avoid allowing our egos to be emotionally wounded by our errors. Perhaps this is what Gibran is telling us as he presents the cornerstone, the most important supporting stone of the temple, representing accomplishment, as low as the lowest stone, our greatest mistake. Learning from our greatest mistakes can propel us toward our highest accomplishments. Without the lowest stone – our greatest mistake – there is no cornerstone – our greatest accomplishment.

The science of yoga tells us to not brood over failures and to quickly let them fade out of our awareness. We may secretly believe that it is "saintly," or a mark of humility, to brood over our failures, as if punishing ourselves will bring us closer to God. We may even believe that the more we mentally punish ourselves, the more holy we are, as if mental punishment means we are learning humility. Truly speaking, brooding or mental punishment may simply be a sign that our ego is out of control. The ego can take great pride in doling out punishment, demonstrating its righteousness! It is not much different from the experience of excess pride and patting ourselves on the back when we have done something well. On a spiritual path, brooding over failure is never recommended as helpful, and certainly does not bring us closer to God.

In the face of mistakes and failure, persistence is invaluable. The late President Richard Nixon said, "A man is not finished when he is defeated, but when he gives up..." In other words, as long as you are trying to change a behavior, you have the potential for success. Failure only comes into the picture when you have stopped trying. There is an old Zen Buddhist saying: "Success in life is falling down nine times and getting up 10 times." When we fail, we need to "...pick ourselves up, dust ourselves off, and start all over again," as the 1936 song by Jerome Kern and Dorothy Fields tells us. We should embrace our failures, learn from them, and move on. Motivational teacher Tony Robbins said, "Success is truly the result of good judgment. Good judgment is the result of experience, and experience is often the result of bad judgment..."!!! Thus, nothing is lost when we make a mistake, or experience a temporary failure. Even so, as we grow in consciousness, we should take steps to avoid serious mistakes, to "avert the danger that is yet to come," as the Upanishads warns us.

Our failures in life can lead us to reexamine what success is, or how we define and understand it, and this examination will help place failures and mistakes in perspective. For example, being denied entry into a fraternity or sorority we desperately want to join can cause us to evaluate why it was so important to gain membership into that society, and if we truly belonged there. Albert Einstein exhorted us to "Try not to be a man of success. Rather, become a man of value..." Exceptional individuals are trying to help us reframe and redefine our understanding of success. This is particularly true as we move through the transformation brought about by spiritual practices -- everything can change for us, including what we define as a successful life. Success should not be based entirely on praise from others -- striving for it should not blind us to what is of value and importance in life.

The best advice on dealing with failure and success is to quickly learn from our failures, move beyond them, and throw ourselves into our pursuits: body, mind, and soul. We should never hold back; we should totally immerse ourselves in life. This has the effect of infusing a spiritual dimension into all our actions. And as AA (Alcoholics Anonymous) tells us, "Don't give up one minute before the miracle happens." Fulfillment could be one moment away, in all its manifestations. We should be innocent. We should avoid judgment. We should simply let go and allow our lives to happen. As Paramhansa Yogananda said, "A saint is a sinner who never gave up!"

Contemplation

1. How would you define failure and success?
2. Think of your biggest failure. What were the repercussions of it -- how did it change you, and how you run your life? What lessons did you learn?
3. It has been said there are two tragedies in life -- not getting your heart's desire... and getting it! Why do you think this is so?
4. If you were created by God, or if you are a son/daughter of God, how can you be imperfect, or a 'failure'?
5. Reflect on the possibility that there is, at one level, no difference between success and mistakes. See each as an action, which differ only in the consequences of the action.

Application

1. Sit down and make a list of every failure and mistake you can think of. Pick the top five and write down three lessons you learned from each, and three ways it changed you. Did you learn more from your successes or your failures? Finally, list three ways or strategies you can use to avoid making this mistake again.

2. Take a new skill to learn and try it -- notice how often you make mistakes. See how intimate it is to the learning process. Can you even imagine not making a mistake? See how they shape the new skill.
3. Discuss this question with another person: can a man or woman who achieves union with God also be a failure? How about a man or woman on the way to union with God? Can either be a failure?
4. Meditation on joy. Visualize a deep sense of joy (perhaps by recalling a joyful activity or scene) centered in your heart. Allow it to expand and infuse itself throughout your whole body -- then into the room in which you were sitting -- then into your house -- to the street on which you live -- to the city, state, and country in which you live, the earth, and the universe. Allow it to soak into everything and everybody. Just stay with this gentle practice for about 15 minutes.

Lesson Fourteen

ON FORGIVENESS

• • • • •

Illumination

"On the wings of forgiveness is carried all other wisdom..."

Honey J. Rubin

A contemporary writer, poet, and motivational speaker, Honey Rubin inspires others to create an Imagine Garden that honors all faith traditions. It is a vision and a prayer for a kinder and gentler world. Honey encourages everyone to engage in the following prayer: "May every mind remember God. May every mind awaken."

"The weak can never forgive. Forgiveness is the attribute of the strong."

Mahatma Gandhi

The 'Great Soul,' Mohandas Gandhi, 1869 – 1948, led the revolt for Indian independence from Britain through a process of nonviolent civil disobedience. He exerted a great influence on Dr. Martin Luther King and others who embraced nonviolent means of protest against established authorities.

> *"...Forgive us our trespasses, as we forgive those who trespass against us."*
>
> ***The Lord's Prayer***

EXAMINATION

Successful engagement with mistakes and failures rests upon your capacity to forgive yourself and others. When we forgive ourselves and others, we clean the slate and start anew. We release ourselves from any self-condemnation in which we engage because of self-created difficulties. Sometimes forgiving ourselves requires only a simple acknowledgement that, in the past, we did the best we could with what we knew at the time. Forgiveness can be an acknowledgment that we did make a mistake, the past is over, and we will try not to make it again.

Forgiveness brings profound purification and clarification. When we forgive, we feel renewed and we return to a state of innocence which is our own original nature.

Forgiveness is an act of love; it is an experience of the Divine working through us. It is an act of generosity, strength, and reparation. It can be exhilarating, blissful even. When we forgive someone else, we release them from bondage, and in the process we, too, move toward freedom. When we forgive, we balance the karmic debts in our lives. We no longer hold ourselves hostage to someone else or consider someone else beholden to us. Recall the feeling of exhilaration you had when you paid off a car loan or, even better, a mortgage. It is so freeing. We can feel lighter than air. Forgiveness can be the basis of mounting joy in our lives.

We can practice forgiveness at every turn; not only giving it, but asking for it. Telling someone that you are sorry and asking them for forgiveness is an act of profound humility. It is a simple and concrete but powerful way to transcend your own ego. When we apologize and ask for forgiveness, we recognize that our ego is not rigid or perfect. We are acknowledging that it is possible for us to make mistakes. When our ego is diminished in this way, we lose some of our identification with our limited sense of self, our self-righteousness. Our ego – the source of bondage and limitation – becomes a little more porous and flexible. We are lighter in an emotional and spiritual way as a result. In short, giving and asking for forgiveness dissolves the barriers and the gulf between individuals. It leads to a sense of connection and to a sense of unity -- it is a doorway to the highest state of consciousness: unity consciousness.

So important is the act of forgiveness that it is included in the Lord's prayer. In this prayer, we ask God to forgive us as we forgive those who trespass against (harm) us. What does this mean? One meaning is that we ask God to forgive us in the *same moment* in which we forgive another. Thus we become the forgiver and the forgiven in the same moment. At the same time in which we forgive someone else from a transgression, perhaps we are forgiven, or are released from the belief that God is upset with us. As we forgive another individual, we elevate their status. We no longer see them as inferior, weak, or of lesser value in relation to us. We see them as being similar to ourselves. In a greater sense, we see them as ourselves. We understand their situation, their intention, and their behavior. We see ourselves in the other and the other person in ourselves. This is a spiritual act, an act of seeing unity among ourselves and others. That is why forgiveness contains God's grace. Grace pours into the spaces in which our differences dissolve.

In our psychotherapy practices, we commonly meet people who tell us they can forgive others, but cannot forgive themselves. Without question, it is a virtue to forgive others, but it requires greater strength to forgive ourselves. And it is of even greater importance to forgive ourselves. The easier it is to forgive ourselves for a wide variety of behaviors, the easier it is to forgive others. The more readily we can forgive ourselves, the more readily we can experience love and compassion for others.

Self-forgiveness is an essential act on the path of spiritual growth. It is impossible to accomplish much on a spiritual path without relinquishing the prison of condemnation that accompanies a lack of self-forgiveness. Each time we forgive ourselves we gain in strength and mastery. Gandhi understood well that forgiveness is a two-way street. As soon as we forgive ourselves for some limitation, we develop the strength to simultaneously forgive others for the same limitation.

Grace pours into the spaces in which our differences dissolve.

I (Vincent) have learned that, as I observe my mistakes and forgive myself, I accept another part of myself. I feel more integrated and whole. Moreover, it then becomes easier to forgive the same mistake made by someone else, and I can see myself in others and appreciate that part of them. So treat yourself like a newborn baby. Let go and love yourself fully. Do you remember the proverb of the prodigal son in the Bible? Recall how readily the father forgave his son, even though the son abandoned his father and squandered a fortune. The father was beside himself with joy when his son returned. Allow yourself to feel that same depth of love for yourself. When you bask in loving self-forgiveness, you are truly on the path to freedom. You will more readily develop a deep empathy and understanding for others, for you will begin to love them as you love yourself.

Forgiving yourself is not getting off the hook; it does not condone irresponsible behavior. Obtaining forgiveness may require that we make amends in order to right a wrong. And as you do, allow your divine nature to flow out of you, through you, and into others. Let yourself be, as St. Francis of Assisi implored, an instrument of God's peace. You deserve love. You deserve to be forgiven: for God has already forgiven you.

Practicing forgiveness may also be beneficial to your physical health. Waltman, et al (2009) studied the physical effects of forgiveness in cardiac patients. Patients who underwent 10 weeks of forgiveness therapy showed fewer anger-recall induced myocardial perfusion defects than a control group receiving counseling about diet and exercise. The authors concluded that forgiveness intervention may be an effective means of reducing anger-induced myocardial ischemia in patients with coronary artery disease. In addition, recent research (Toussaint, et al, 2016) with 148 young adults found that the tendency to use forgiveness was a strong independent predictor of mental and physical health, regardless of the amount of stress they had experienced in life. These results are part of a growing body of research which indicates that having a forgiving nature and engaging in forgiveness behavior brings both lasting physical and mental health benefits for the one who forgives.

Contemplation

1. Your job in life, according to spirituality, is simple - you are to purify the mind, attain freedom, live in bliss, and evolve. Right now, think about how forgiving someone can assist you with these processes.
2. Reflect on the last time you forgave someone. How long ago was it? Recall how it felt.
3. Why do you think it appears to be much easier to forgive others than forgive ourselves? What beliefs do you harbor that prevent you from forgiving yourself? Is there any condition where you think you could never forgive? Why? What does a lack of forgiveness do to someone? What does it do to you?
4. Recall the proverb in the New Testament (Luke 15: 11-32) of the Prodigal Son. Why was the father so overjoyed at the return of this son that he prepared a feast for him, and met him on the road to welcome him on the way to the feast? Why was the father seemingly more pleased with the prodigal son than with his eldest son, who was loyal and worked hard for his father throughout his life?

Application

1. Practice this Tibetan Buddhist meditation of loving kindness.

   Choose a quiet place and sit comfortably. Gently say to yourself, "May I be filled with loving kindness; may I be peaceful and at ease; may I be happy." Gently repeat these phrases. As you do, visualize yourself as an innocent child in God's arms. Feel a healing, loving radiance engulf you. Practice this for about 20 minutes.

2. Sit down and write a letter to someone who you hurt and ask that person to forgive you.
3. Mentally go through your entire life experience and think of a significant wrong that you experienced. Now practice the loving kindness meditation, this time with the person who wronged you as the focus.
4. Brainstorm a list of all the situations you have experienced in your life where you have not forgiven someone. Looking over the list, how does this make you feel?

LESSON FIFTEEN

HUMILITY

● ● ● ● ●

ILLUMINATION

> *"The first quality or virtue we have to develop before we aspire to have God is humility... you have in fact to unlearn what you have learned. You must become simple, unsophisticated, and childlike..."*
>
> ***Papa Ramdas***

Swami Ramdas, 1884-1963, was an Indian saint and disciple of the great Ramana Maharishi. After living in solitude in a cave, he had the experience that all was God. His devotees established an ashram for him in Kerala, India, in 1931.

EXAMINATION

Shortly after I (Vincent) embarked on my spiritual path, I spent an afternoon in a large meditation hall in an ashram in the Catskill Mountains, and I prayed to God for an answer to the following question: "Why am I here on earth?" The answer came swiftly and strongly: "To learn patience and humility." Believe me when I say that I had hoped for a different answer. For one thing, I was tired of learning patience. Growing up in New York City quickly forces one to exercise patience to a seemingly unending degree, by waiting on countless lines, driving in constant traffic, and otherwise experiencing oneself as a small, insignificant person in a seething sea of humanity. I felt I had all the patience I needed. Humility, on the other hand, was a virtue I did not completely understand. I knew it had something to do with 'having your ego busted,' which is not a pleasant experience. I knew I did not need more unpleasant experiences. As with the quality of patience, I was disappointed at the prospect of discovering that I needed to learn more humility. I had enough disappointment in life, and did not think learning more humility was really necessary. Despite my initial reactions to this inner reply to my question, I continue working on these lessons to this very day.

Much has been written on humility, and we could write at length on this subject. Given that the lessons in this book emphasize the gist of spiritual truths to be contemplated and savored, we prefer to focus on the role of humility on the spiritual path. Humility, for me, is about learning that everyone and everything is another form of God, and that God exists in infinite forms. What this means is that, as much as I like to feel 'special,' 'different,' 'superior,' 'set apart from,' and 'unique,' it just isn't so. How we differ from each other on the superficial level of the personality, or differ from each other in other ways – physical features, educational attainment, financial accomplishment, etc. – is inconsequential when it comes to realizing the Self. Thus, I have been faced with learning that what I "think" about who I am in terms of worldly characteristics is irrelevant. Realizing the Self is not about how 'special' the particular ego, personality, and worldly circumstances that comprise 'me' may appear to be.

Developing this attitude or point of view is not easy, as it seems to be completely opposite to everything one needs to do to 'get ahead' from a career point of view. To progress in a career, we have to market ourselves, which means establishing our own 'brand.' We market ourselves by promoting our 'unique features' on social networking sites, on our personal websites or blogs, and by writing papers, giving talks, spicing up our resumes, and getting our names in front of the public whenever possible. Clearly, humility is not a valued commodity in the professional world. In a job interview, for example, acting "simple, unsophisticated, and childlike" does not seem to be a valuable "winning strategy." Therefore, it is a reasonable question to ask just how one develops humility, while moving ahead professionally.

The answer lies in the ability to separate the personality level from a higher or deeper level, the level of who you really are. On the personality level, it is essential to play the game of marketing oneself and play it well, by appearing confident, intelligent, and proud of one's accomplishments. But, at the same time, one can play this game while remaining in a state of understanding that everything that is happening – while one tries to market oneself- is occurring because God wills it, and that we are simply individuals playing the role God has assigned to us in each moment, as best we can. And if that role includes demonstrating our prowess and showing off our skills and accomplishments, then we do it to the fullest, all the while realizing that God is the Source of all of our energy, our intellect, and our actions. God acts through us, even in challenging interview situations!

When it comes to Realizing the Self, the individual personality with which I continue to identify can exist just as it is. The qualities of my personality, or any personality, as we said, have little to do with Self-Realization. The same is true regarding our degree of 'knowledge' or lack of 'knowledge' about spirituality. The Great Beings also say that a storehouse of knowledge accumulated over many years can often be a great obstacle in understanding the Truth. Thus, knowledge of spiritual or philosophical texts is no guarantee of Self-Realization – they may actually be a hindrance. Nor is a bubbly, outward interpersonal style such a guarantee. A person with little or no knowledge of spiritual or philosophical texts and an introverted, shy interpersonal style may have the same ability in reaching Self-Realization, if not greater ability. Children, who have much less to unlearn about themselves and the world compared with adults, may have an advantage toward achieving Self-Realization. All of the Great Beings say the Truth is simple: so simple a child can grasp it.

Learning humility is a matter of refining our character through developing virtues such as patience, truthfulness, and dependability, and learning to identify increasingly with the Great Self. One way to progress in changing identification from the small self to the Self of All involves renouncing the sense of "Doership." The ego, or small self, likes to believe it is in control and performs various actions all day long. It likes to think that it makes plans for the future, engages in numerous activities, and formulates decisions, some of which turn out "right" and some of which turn out "wrong." "Doing things" and "making things happen" is the way the ego feels in control. The change in identification that needs to happen involves an understanding that the Self is in control, that God is the Doer of all actions, functioning through each of us. While the mind will likely not understand the concept that we do not "do" things we clearly appear to be doing, from the point of view of the Self, God acts through each of us. We can relax with the knowledge that 'God is in charge,' as the saying goes, and we are simply the 'Witness' to and not the "Doer" of actions.

On a spiritual journey it is the ego, along with its partner, the mind, which interferes with attaining humility. The ego does not want to be humble; the ego wants to control and expand. The ego likes to be 'right.' The ego wants to be seen as special, better than, and does all it can to grow in size and power. (Most of us can readily recognize an egotistical person whose ego is well out of control). Moreover, the ego tends to feel it knows virtually everything, and that there is nothing more to be learned. If the ego were left in charge over the course of our lives, we would experience little or no change in our attitudes towards ourselves, others, or the world. There would be no inner growth or development. The ego thinks it is fine just as it is. Certainly, the ego does not want to give up anything required for a spiritual awakening, much less permanent enlightenment. The ego feels that to give up anything means it is losing, becoming weak, and shrinking. In the language of the ego, experiences that causes it to shrink are for 'losers.'

Cultivating humility is a powerful way to neutralize the ego. Jesus said the first shall be last and the last shall be first when referring to humility. Milarepa, the Buddhist Sage, has counseled us to "Take the lowest place and you shall reach the highest." Putting others before ourselves is an act of making the ego subservient to the higher Self, which we share with all of humanity and the rest of creation. When we practice humility in relation to others, we shed our sense of being special, being entitled, and feeling superior. But this does not mean we view ourselves as lower, weaker, inferior, subservient, and lesser than others. When we think of ourselves as "less than" or inferior to others, we are demonstrating a kind of false humility, which is the flip side of egotism. Proclaiming to be humbler than others is simply another ego trip. True humility is about eliminating all comparisons with others in the first place. In fact, true humility involves a shifting identification from the egoic sense – the sense that we know and 'do' everything – to identification with the Truth, the Inner Self. When there is true humility, we have surrendered our sense of 'doership,' the false notion that we are always in charge and in control, and that everything that happens in our lives has happened because we have willed it to be so.

All of the great spiritual traditions emphasize humility, purity, and truth. The science of yoga tells us that humility is among the highest of all virtues, including simplicity, wisdom, and emptiness.

What does it mean to become unsophisticated and childlike? Adults see children as innocent, naïve to the ways of the world, and in need of constant adult guidance. Of course, to a degree, children do need a lot of help and protection from adults. When a child wants to make friends with another child, she asks one simple question: "Do you want to play?" If the second child responds "Yes," and starts to play with the first child, the two children are friends. As simple as that. In asking another child to play, the first child did not make a careful assessment of the second child's familial roots, cultural background, physical appearance, financial stability, educational level, and style of dress before making the request. She simply asked to play.

Young children render very little judgment in their choices of befriending others. If they enjoy a shared activity, they are friends and enjoy being with each other. This is humility: the full acceptance of another individual without the interfering judgments of the mind and the acculturation process which suggest our friends must meet specific criteria.

Unlearning the many concepts we have learned about classifying and categorizing other persons before we can accept and love them is an essential milestone on the spiritual path. The more easily you experience love for others, the more you can expand the number of persons of all different types for whom you can feel love, and the greater your attainment on a spiritual path. Love, after all, is at the heart of spiritual accomplishment, so the great Masters tell us.

A simple way to practice humility is to see God's perfection everywhere: perfection in oneself, perfection in others, and perfection in nature. See the hand of God in all that happens, whether the mind considers some events 'good' and others 'bad.'

Humility is a quality that promotes spiritual growth, as it dissolves our limiting ego and expands our conscious identification beyond the narrow confines of the individual person/body. Amma, the contemporary Indian saint, tells us that "where there is humility, there (God's) grace will reach effortlessly" (Matruvani, May 2012, Vol. 23, No. 9, p 2-5). She adds that where there is humility, wisdom and discrimination grow. Over time, these qualities ultimately point us toward liberation and freedom. We empty ourselves of "all that is not God," as St. Thomas Aquinas noted. When we forget ourselves, we remember God and submit to his will, to the TAO, to the Way of things. Being humble is an orientation to life. It engenders a sense of respect for all living beings. It helps us let go of our selfishness, as we live and let live.

Contemplation

1. The Chinese character for humility is also the same character for emptiness. How do you see being inwardly empty or unpossessing a virtue akin to humility?
2. Webster's dictionary defines humility as freedom from pride and arrogance. How do you think pride and arrogance are developed? How can you overcome a tendency toward these two traits?
3. What is your view of humility? What indications of humility do you show, according to your definition?
4. Thomas Merton, the great Cistercian monk and Mystic, says that the man of humility can do great things well, as he is unconcerned about and doesn't waste energy defending his own reputation and interests. What do you see as the benefits of humility in your life? How can humility make you strong?
5. Describe the humblest person you ever met. What impact did this person have on you?

Application

1. Journey to a library or bookstore. Look around you and realize all that you do not know—can never know—compared with what you do know. Note the feeling that this gives you.
2. Perform an act of humility over the next 24 hours, and write down and discuss its impact on you. List your own obstacles to cultivating humility.

3. Visit a natural area, such as a forest, a meadow, or a beach. Explore your own feelings of humility in connection with the beauty you see around you, its vastness, and the endless manifestations of creation.
4. Sometime over the next 24 hours, deliberately be obedient or subservient, or acquiesce to someone in some small way. Be aware of your egoic reaction to not being the boss, or being in control. What does your reaction inform you about the size of your ego?
5. Tell someone close to you what you have learned from them and how this learning changed your life for the better. Notice how you feel afterward.
6. Close your eyes and sit quietly for about one minute. Practice some bodily relaxation - and then visualize yourself surrendering all you have: all your efforts, your body, your mind, and all that you possess to God. See yourself totally submitting to God's will, becoming an instrument of God's peace. See yourself giving selflessly to others -- just stay with this gentle awareness...
7. Reducing the tendency toward identification with being the "doer" of actions can be achieved by not being attached to the consequences of actions. Think about your expectations for how you intend your actions to turn out. Can you practice performing actions without expectations for how they will turn out?

LESSON SIXTEEN

EMBRACING CHANGE

• • • • •

ILLUMINATION

"Change is life. Without change, there would be no growth, no understanding, no relating, and no surprises. We are, by nature, changing beings. Still, we seem to fear and resist it more than any other aspect of life..."

Leo Buscalia

Leo, 1924-1998, was a faculty member of the Department of Special Education at the University of Southern California. His lectures on LOVE turned into a book by that title. A highly rated lecturer on PBS, 11 million copies of his books were sold by the time of his death in 1998.

"Only that which is real never changes..."

Shankara

A philosopher and theologian who lived in the 8th century CE, Shankara unified the major tenets of Hinduism. Considered the founder of Advaita (non-dual) Vedanta, he wrote hundreds of philosophical works. He established monastic schools and traveled extensively throughout India.

Examination

There are few people alive who welcome change. Most of us try to avoid change or at least hope to avoid it. True, some of us can tolerate change, but most of us simply don't like it. Psychologists, who are considered to be "change agents"—that is, professionals who help clients make important changes in their lives—know full well that most people who come for therapy truly do not want to change anything about their lives. They simply want some support and validation about how they go about making decisions in their everyday lives, regardless of how well things are working out. When psychologists suggest making a behavior change, many people start to squirm in their seats and try to change the topic. Truth be told, there are those of us working as psychologists who also are not crazy about making changes.

The kind of problems that motivate us to work with a therapist tend to keep us stuck. Dealing with our problems challenges the status quo. That is, if we are to resolve the problems, we must face the fact that we need to change in some fundamental way. Yet we often will not, or perhaps cannot change. Consciously or unconsciously, we all seem to resist change, even if we are in great pain. Biologically, this resistance may be a psychological maneuver to conserve energy. From a spiritual perspective, resistance may be a kind of test of our seriousness about transforming ourselves on the spiritual path.

Contemplating a change of job, relationship partner, or a place to live can be somewhat uncomfortable. We simply don't know whether a change will lead to an improvement or will make things worse, and nobody wants to try to change something only to see things become worse! Most of us try to hold onto what little we have for dear life, out of fear that a change can lead to things in our lives becoming worse.

Yet, if we look around, we cannot deny that change is a fact of life. While some things in life change slowly, other things change more quickly. For example, our personalities do not seem to change very much over the span of several years, but many parts of our bodies change tremendously over the same period of time. The lining of our stomach changes every 24 hours. A red blood cell in our body lives about 100 days until it is replaced. In a span of 365 days, we essentially have a very different body, from the cellular level on up. Over the course of many years, people come into our lives and people leave our lives. We eventually see many of our loved ones move away and pass away, including our parents and older relatives, our friends, our neighbors, and our coworkers. Neighborhoods go through transformations. Prices go up and down. The map of the world changes dramatically over the course of only 100 years.

We face changes our ancestors relegated to the realm of science fiction. They never had to worry about their jobs being taken over by robots, or about artificial intelligence possibly determining the course of human events on planet earth. Over the past few decades, climate has changed markedly. And as time goes by, we must admit that we don't look the same as we did when we were younger.

So the question is: if change is going to occur whether or not we like it, shouldn't we embrace it? After all, the Dalai Lama suggests that everyone try to visit a new place at least once per year, and following this suggestion requires us to make, at least, very small changes in our lives. There are two compelling reasons to embrace change. One reason is that if we try to resist change, sooner or later we are going to pay a big price for our resistance. For example, there are people who try hard not to grow up. They do not want to leave home, get a job, and start new relationships. Instead, they continue to live with their parents in the home in which they grew up. They pride themselves on their loyalty in taking care of their parents. For some of these individuals, serving as caretakers for their parents consumes their entire lives to such a degree that they do not make new friends or forge new relationships outside the nuclear family. When the aged parent(s) finally passes away, the adult child is crushed and not equipped to fend for himself. Deep depression sets in. A feeling of abandonment overtakes all other feelings. He no longer has anything to live for. As difficult as it is to experience the loss of a parent, it is far easier if we have created a new family and a new life for ourselves while the parent is still alive. Psychological research demonstrates that those who are flexible, who are willing to shift their perceptions and embrace change, live longer, happier, and more productive lives.

A second reason to embrace change is that at some point in life, we might admit that our existing lifestyle is not leading us to happiness. No matter how much material success we have, at some point it is seen wanting. While we may have enviable lives from a material point of view, we continue to experience sadness and depression, jealousy, envy, despair, fear, and a myriad of other negative feelings which indicate we have much to accomplish in life, from a spiritual standpoint. As we assess our spiritual growth, or lack of it, we are forced to conclude that we need to make some changes in how we spend our time, what goals we wish to pursue, what we most value in life, how we relate to others, and how we relate to ourselves.

To embark upon a spiritual program is to throw yourself into flux and sometimes marked, change. Over the years, I (Vincent) have had to reevaluate and change everything, from my physical posture, diet, sleep pattern, habitual thought patterns, and ways of relating to others, to other aspects of my life. These changes have not been easy, but resisting the changes have made things more difficult. I have found that if I can keep myself from evaluating changes as good or bad, fortunate or unfortunate, and positive or negative, I can accept them more readily. For example, in my spiritual community, like many spiritual communities, regular change is almost a built-in aspect of our practice, which prepares us well for when change is required in other parts of our lives. Our ability to accept and embrace change can assist us in making substantial progress in our spiritual journeys.

In professional practice, I often assist people who wish to make changes in their habits and customs. When we change, we become flexible, and do not feel bound by the "way things are" or "have to be." Making even the smallest of changes – visiting new places and restaurants, or striking up a new friendship – can be a freeing experience, which allows us to develop the confidence to accept what comes in life.

There is no question that life on the physical and psychological dimensions appears to consist of constant change. Thus, it is a paradox when the great sage, Shankara, tells us in no uncertain words that only the unchanging is real. Are all the changing aspects of ourselves and our world not real? Are we living in an illusion? Shankara offers a powerful, provocative statement. He tells us that only the eternal is real, not that which is changing constantly. Yet, all we see is constant movement – creation, maintenance, and destruction – wherever we look. For example, we move into an apartment or build a house, we live in it, perhaps raise a family in it, and ultimately leave it for some other place. This constant change (sometimes changing slowly and sometimes changing quickly) over a period of many years is what we consider "our story," or our "personal story."

If we become more discerning, however, we realize that this constant flux occurs against a background of absolutely no change; and that is precisely why we are able to see and experience the changes in our lives. A good movie takes place on an unchanging screen. An intriguing show occurs on the backdrop of an unchanging stage. In the same manner, the drama of life as we know it occurs on the unchanging background of Pure Consciousness. The latter is also referred to as the Supreme Witness, the Perceiver, or Awareness.

In the Hindu philosophical language, the two aspects of life - the relative, or changing, and the absolute, or unchanging - both exist simultaneously, and herein lies the paradox. The changing and the changeless are represented in the Hindu tradition by the gods, Shiva and Shakti. Shiva is the unchanging, all-pervading Stillness, the ground of creation, Supreme Consciousness in perfect repose. Shakti, his wife, is the ever-changing, energetic, activating power of Supreme Consciousness. She is sometimes depicted as a great dancer: a Cosmic Dancer, in fact. Shiva and Shakti are husband and wife, the masculine and feminine principle. Although they appear as two, in reality they are one: different aspects of a Unitary Supreme Being.

Why is it important to think about this? Change in life is a given. Shakti will do Her dance. Life will go on, our personal stories will unfold, and change will emerge as part of the natural order of things. But if we view change as "bad," as "wrong," as "unnecessary," we may waste a lot of energy thinking that we need to undo things or fix things. Even worse, we may think we have "messed up" when things change.

The spiritual challenge for us when it comes to dealing with change involves acceptance: to take life as it comes, go with things as they roll, and find peace with the numerous challenges that life gives us; while, at the same time, remaining firmly established in the unchanging field of the Absolute. What does this mean? First, understand that you are not "your story." After all, "your story" in life could have been written in so many different ways. You might have selected a different college major, taken different jobs, found different friends, moved to different places, and acquired different relationship partners. By understanding that you are not defined by or as "your story," you start to shift your identification to being "Pure Consciousness," or "Awareness" itself. Second, when the stress involved with change is getting you down, immerse yourself in your Inner Being. Take a breath, close your eyes, and go inside yourself. Rest in your Inner Self, the Pure Being. Sometimes, taking only one complete breath in a conscious manner, shifts your entire internal state.

Remember, 'Pure Being' does not change – this is why you can rest in this space of awareness - but the process of 'Becoming' is all about change. We need to always remain consciously aware of and identified with our true identity as Pure Being – as awareness and consciousness - even as we deal with what becomes of us in life: our 'story'. Spirituality and spiritual practices provide us the anchor to focus on the 'Absolute,' or the eye of the hurricane as we rise to the challenges of our changing lives.

There is yet another paradox we will face sometime in the spiritual journey. If we wish to become free and attain the state of enlightenment, we must be willing to change all that we think we understand about the natural order of things. We will have to consider that life is different than how we always thought it was. In contrast, we will find ourselves directing our focus to the Absolute, which is the undistorted, essential nature of our being. This is a process that likely will occur slowly, step by step. Ultimately, this change does not require any particular effort; rather, it is the opposite of effort - we allow change to happen - we allow ourselves to sink back into our true changeless nature. For, as the great mystic St. Theresa of Avila has said, only God is changeless... if we are to rest in the Union with God, we must ourselves embrace the changeless. If we don't change, we simply harden. The truth is **there is no other way.**

Contemplation

1. What are you most afraid of changing and why?
2. Imagine a life with no change at all. How would that affect us? What would things be like in 20 years?
3. Think of a flowing river. There is a saying that it is impossible to set foot into the same river twice. What is the meaning of this statement? In other words, if you set foot into a river at one time, pull out your foot, and put your foot back into the

river, what is the same about the river and what is different about the river? How are we human beings similar to droplets of water in the river?

4. The Koran says, "God will not change the condition of men until they change what is in themselves..." Christians are fond of saying that God helps those that help themselves. The 12 steps of AA tell us that God removes our shortcomings, not us. What are your thoughts on change in spiritual matters? Do you believe that it involves willpower and effort?
5. Meister Eckhart, the great mystic, has said, "Wood does not change the fire into itself, but the fire changes the wood into itself. So we are changed into God, that we shall know him as he is." This is a profoundly provocative statement: the ultimate change comes from the divine, not us. As Osho has said, "To know the real, you first must be the real. Only the same can know the same." The Vedas echo the same truth -- what we see, we become. The divine changes us into the divine! What are your thoughts on this?

APPLICATION

1. Pick something simple to change. For example, you might eat at a new restaurant, travel to a new place, or initiate a conversation with someone with whom you have never previously spoken. Notice your emotional reaction to it and any resistance you experience. Did you feel a sense of new freedom or power? Do you feel better able to try additional new endeavors?
2. Meditate for 15 minutes and notice what changed in you and what did not.

3. Try to change someone else's behavior, and note your experiences. Were you successful?
4. Many elderly people state that they feel the same in some ways as they did when they were young – despite the fact that they may be physically challenged. Why do they say this? What do you think has not changed for them over the course of their lives?
5. Since the dawn of planet earth billions of years ago, what is it that has not changed? Can you describe it? Write down your ideas.

Lesson Seventeen

PURPOSE

• • • • •

Illumination

"Those who have failed to work toward the truth have missed the purpose of living."

Siddhartha Gautama Buddha

Siddhartha Gautama, Lord Buddha, taught in India between the 6th and 4th centuries BCE. He is the enlightened founder of Buddhism. After being ordered to live a life of seclusion, he ventured out into the world, realized the inevitable suffering of life, and led an ascetic life, determined to rid the world of all suffering.

Examination

There is a point on the spiritual journey when a seeker begins to inquire about his priorities in life, and asks himself questions such as "What do I want to accomplish over the course of my life?" If all you cared about in life was having access to great drugs, sex, power, or money, you likely would not be reading this lesson. True seekers want to know why they are in this world and what they were meant to accomplish. Learning about who you truly are and your relationship to God is perhaps your greatest priority of life if you are a true seeker, and it is this curiosity that likely has attracted grace in your life.

At a certain point in the spiritual journey, the primary intention of one's life needs to be to discover your true identity and true home. For many of us, the intention does not need to be stated, but merely recognized as a goal that has been foremost in our hearts for much of our lives. Purpose is important when embarking on a spiritual journey.

When the Buddha discusses the purpose of living, he implies that life should have an aim, a direction, or a goal, as the Webster's Dictionary definition of the word 'purpose' indicates. On close examination you might ask what you have accomplished in your life without an intention or a purpose. If you have some degree of proficiency in your chosen field, whether you are a bookkeeper, mother, correctional officer, engineer, or physician, you likely formed an intention to dedicate yourself to learning your craft and gaining some degree of proficiency. The same is true of other endeavors in life, such as athletics, music, or culinary arts.

There is a saying that 'practice makes perfect.' Spiritual practices are essential for progress in the spiritual arena. Note that the Buddha discussed "working toward the truth," not simply thinking about the truth. He referred to the importance of putting one's effort into aligning oneself with the Truth, or becoming established in the Truth as the purpose of life.

Within a year or so after starting spiritual practices, I (Vincent) formed an intention to remain a spiritual seeker for the rest of my life. By that time, I had sufficient experiences to convince me that there was nothing on this earth of greater value than pursuing Self-Realization. Although, at times, my intention sometimes is stronger and, at other times, is not as strong, my overall intention to pursue Self-Realization throughout my life never changes. This does not mean that I have abandoned any of my family or professional responsibilities or my general enjoyment of life. In fact, my family life and professional life have benefitted substantially. But my ongoing intention is the motivating force for me to pursue spiritual practices routinely, and to know that I pursue them for a particular purpose or end result.

What does it mean to miss the purpose of living? Is it like missing the bus? I think the answer is yes. There is a certain point in life in which one realizes that the accumulation of money, friends, possessions, and experiences is fine, but that something more must be available and possible. More satisfying and permanent goals of life may contain attributes such as Wisdom, Contentment, Peace, Bliss, and Harmony. What goal(s) can be higher, or greater?

Gautama Buddha was not the only one to suggest that purpose is important in life. Elizabeth Kubler-Ross tells us to get in touch with our inner silence and to come to the realization that everything in our lives has a purpose. Ralph Waldo Emerson tells us that the purpose of life is for man to acquaint himself with himself. Sufiism takes this point a step further and tells us that the purpose of life is to unlearn what has been learned, and to remember what has been forgotten -- our divine nature, the

Self. A number of the great spiritual traditions tell us to align ourselves with the divine purpose and live in harmony with God's will. Aristotle tells us, "Happiness is the meaning and the purpose of life, the whole aim and end of human existence." Modern psychology would agree that discovering and fulfilling our purpose leads to self-actualization, and supports our mental, emotional, and physical health. A major psychological task in life is to discover meaning in our lives, to arrive at an understanding of our purpose, and to devote our lives to fulfilling it.

Although the Buddha exhorts us to work toward accomplishing life's purpose, there is an entirely different way to look at purpose in life. Simply put, this philosophy states that there is no purpose in life. Zen Buddhism in particular extols the aimless life, the life that has no ultimate goal or objective. In this view, life is simply a process to be lived. Any meaning we impute or attach to it is arbitrary and an add-on. The purposeless life, however, is not conceptualized as a depressing state of affairs. When asked about the meaning of life during an interview with journalist Bill Moyers, the great mythologist Joseph Campbell retorted, "What is the meaning of a flea?" Does anything have inherent meaning? Is not meaning something that we construct based on ideas, beliefs, attitudes - the thinking process itself?

For Zen Buddhism, the aimless life is exemplified by hidden glens of beautiful wildflowers – glorious, for no one to see; rivers meandering aimlessly, with no point to their wandering; the ocean, ceaselessly washing the sand, flowing back onto itself, to no end. In this manner of thinking, life is its own purpose: it simply is. It does not need to be explained, defined, or interpreted by the human mind. As you grow on the spiritual path to higher states of expanded consciousness, your need for purpose or meaning may begin to fade as you become more and more fulfilled from within your own Inner Being. You may no longer feel compelled to discover a 'purpose in life.' As the great saint Nisargadatta Maharaj has put it:

"You have a purpose only as long as you are not complete; until then, completeness, perfection, is the purpose. But when you are complete in yourself, fully integrated within and without, then you enjoy the universe, you do not labor at it..."

Thus, the fulfillment of the spiritual path is itself the purpose; and once it is realized, there is purpose no more.

Contemplation

1. Eleanor Roosevelt said that the purpose of life is to live it; to taste experience to the utmost; to reach out for newer and richer experience. How are you living your life? Are you settling for something less than you could?
2. The Sufi saying noted above tells us to unlearn what has been learned. This implies that we need to engage in deconditioning and access our true Self. What do you see are the benefits of unlearning everything you have been conditioned by thus far in life?
3. "Your sole business in life is to attain God realization. All else is useless and worthless..." Thus spoke Sivananda. Do you think he is right? If so, what is your plan to accomplish this lofty goal?

Application

1. Write down your own purpose, intention, aim, or goal in life -- devise several strategies to help you realize your goal.

2. Examine yourself and your life for behaviors that are at cross purposes with your goals, and devise a plan to reverse them.
3. Spend the next 24 hours in the state of aimlessness -- just stay in the moment, be in the process of life, and do not think about achieving any results or attaining any goals. When you perform any activities or actions, let go of looking for any specific results. Journal your experiences when you are finished.

LESSON EIGHTEEN

ON PRAYER

• • • • •

ILLUMINATION

"Many cry to God, but not with the voice of the soul, but with the voice of the body; only the cry of the heart, of the soul, reaches God."
"Whether we realize it or not, prayer is the encounter of God's thirst and ours."

St. Augustine

Augustine was a 4th century philosopher and writer who was Bishop of Hippo in northern Africa. He is known for having written *Confessions*, *City of God*, and other works.

"Direct all your prayers to one thing only, which is to conform your will perfectly to the Divine will..."

Mother Teresa

A contemporary saint, Mother Teresa, 1910-1997, a Roman Catholic sister and missionary, devoted much of her life to assisting the poor in the slums of Calcutta and elsewhere. She founded the order of the Missionaries of Charity and won a Nobel Peace Prize.

Examination

Who among us does not wish to learn to pray effectively? Who would not like to have an inside track, a direct pipeline to the Divine? The Saints tell us that God is constantly listening to our prayers, is open for business 24 hours per day, and is always there for us. But there are secrets to learning effective prayer, secrets I did not know when I started on a spiritual path.

The first secret is described by St. Augustine: "... only the cry of the heart, of the soul, reaches God." What is the cry of the heart? The cry of the heart is our deepest yearning, our fondest desire, our sincerest plea for God's love, assistance, and guidance. "Amma" (Mata Amritanandamayi) says that the vital element of prayer is humility. Prayer, she tells us, is a state in which we stand humbly before God with our head bowed in surrender, with the conviction that God is everything and we (our ego sense) are nothing. Prayers that are heartfelt and come from a strong desire for communication with God are most effective in their results. Consider the following prayer for help when a relationship is ending. "Oh Lord, you are all-knowing and all-giving. Help me overcome my fear of feeling lonely; allow me to find the means to feel your Divine presence with me at all times and in all places." When we pray with a fervent desire to let the light of God into our lives, we are communicating with Her.

While research efforts probably cannot be used to validate that 'only the cry of the heart, of the soul, reaches God,' recent research results do indicate that the attitude with which we pray has an effect on our psychological health. In 2014, Dr. Chris Ellison and his colleagues evaluated the results of 1,714 volunteers who participated in the Baylor Religion Survey. They found that people who pray to a God they perceive as loving and protective are less likely to experience anxiety-related disorders—worry, fear, self-consciousness, social anxiety, and obsessive compulsive behavior—compared to people who pray but don't really expect to receive any comfort or protection from God. Thus, it seems that the attitude people hold toward God and the quality of the relationship they perceive themselves to have with Him affect their psychological health. That is, if they feel He will hear and respond to their heartfelt communication with Him, the less likely they are to experience anxiety-related problems.

A second secret is based on Augustine's quote: "Prayer is the encounter of God's thirst and ours." What this quote suggests is that God thirsts for us as we thirst for him: we thirst for each other. We want the closest relationship possible with each other. This is an incredible concept, that the desire for contact with God is not a one-way street. Rather, God also wants a relationship with us. The attitude we tend to hold in prayer is that each of us is "the doer," praying to a second party, God, ostensibly listening in a distant location. From the point of view that each of us is already united with God, it can be said that God is both the one who prays and the one who receives the prayer. In a moment of deep prayer, we merge with the Divine, and it becomes impossible to discern who is praying and who is being prayed to.

When we pray, we may sense intuitively that we are out of alignment with the Divine. In fact, we may be prompted to pray as we realize that things in our lives are not proceeding as we would like. We might feel temporarily disconnected, so to speak, from the Source of our energy and power. We seek to be as closely aligned as possible, so that God will know our intentions, and will intercede and help us. Prayer is a powerful use of energy which brings us into alignment with the Divine. When we pray, we are connecting.

Prayer can be formal or informal, vocal or subvocal. We can engage in intercessory prayer for others, or petitionary prayer for ourselves. Some forms of prayer are very similar to meditation, generally known as contemplative prayer. Sometimes prayer does not involve asking for favors or assistance, but is simply a desire to feel the Divine Presence. Whatever the form of prayer, the process always involves a transcending of the ego, a letting go of the wants, needs, desires, and notions of the small self.

All the great spiritual traditions instruct us to pray for God's will, not simply our own to be done, as Mother Teresa tells us. Does that mean that it is not OK to pray for our individual needs: a new and better relationship, help for our loved ones, assistance with an illness, or guidance that we may do well on a difficult test in school? I do not believe that Mother Teresa is suggesting that these prayers are in any way inadequate. But what she appears to be suggesting is that we ask for God's will to be done in a particular situation, and not simply ask God to do what we want Her to do. In other words, God is not merely an extension of our ego or egoic desires.

Our knowledge of what is needed in any situation, while well-intentioned, may likely be incomplete. When we turn our will over to God, we are requesting that because the Divine has complete knowledge (omniscience) of a situation, the perfect outcome occurs at the right time. It has been said that if you want to make God laugh, then tell Her your plans. Sometimes our prayers can appear like requests that God rubber stamp our action plan for the future, and we hope God will agree that we have developed an effective plan. After Jesus of Nazareth first pleaded with God to consider sparing his life, he transcended his personal wants and fears and acceded to the Divine will. Shakespeare said we must follow -- not force -- Providence. He appeared to be making the point that prayer is not exactly taking out our wish list and asking God to fulfill it. Rama Krishna has told us to be "like a dead leaf in the divine wind -- allow yourself to be blown anywhere."

We are advised to be open to the ways in which God would respond to our prayers, regardless of whether the response is the one we would have chosen ourselves (with our egoic sense). The great mystic, Meister Eckhart, counsels us to "Remain still, and let God act and speak in you." Lao Tzu, the great Taoist master, says, "Do nothing by the self-will, but rather conform to heaven's will, and everything will be done for you..." Prayer, in a single stroke, accomplishes that which the divine energy and life desires. It is a powerful form of communication with the subtlest aspect of existence. In prayer, we can set our ego aside and join forces with infinite power. We then allow that power to act as a lightning rod through our body and minds, transforming all in our path. In prayer, we are like a rechargeable battery pack that has been plugged into its power source. After plugging in, God's energy can be directed to act on the relationship problem, the illness, the difficult test, and other life conditions.

The repeated practice of prayer slowly leads to ego detoxification and can eventually lead to a state of egolessness. When you pray, you are entering into a state of surrender, a state of acceptance, a state of acquiescence to the Divine will. When you are praying, you are no longer in the purview of the ego -- you have asked to enter the state of the Divine. One method of prayer begins by invoking God's presence (e.g., saying "In the name of the Father, the Son, and Holy Spirit" for Christians), stating our situation or need to God in a clear and succinct manner, and then sitting silently in God's presence for a time. We conclude by thanking Him for Divine assistance and extending an offer of gratitude. We then patiently wait to discern how God's response to our prayer becomes manifest.

Prayer helps us not only in the spiritual dimension, but in other ways as well. There is a substantial and growing body of research on how prayer affects our physical health as well as our psychological health. Dr. Harold Koenig (2015), at Duke University, reviewed over 1500 research studies on the effects of prayer on the physical body. His review found that persons who prayed regularly had lower blood pressure and stronger immune systems, and coped with stress better than those who did not pray regularly.

My experience with prayer is that sometimes there are immediate responses in that I have found something I was missing, remembered something important, or had a potential problem disappear. At other times, the responses to prayers seem to be years in the making, and not apparent for a long period of time. Perhaps as importantly, after prayer I have the feeling I am not alone in having to deal with a problem. God and I are 'partners' solving the problem together. During and after prayer, I sometimes feel what I would call a delicious energy state, letting me know that I am being heard and nurtured.

The longer or more frequently that you pray, the greater the chance that you will go beyond the thinking process itself and rest in the reality beyond words that is God -- the peace that passes all understanding. The great teacher Maharishi Mahesh Yogi has told us, "The thought of God finds fulfillment in its own extinction." When prayer is sincere and one-pointed (focused like a laser), you achieve an experience of what you are saying, on a verbal or thought level, to God. Eventually all thoughts, all words, and all mental experiences must fall away, and you come to rest in the Divine union. This is the inevitable result of a life of prayer. The Koran says the Lord shall never forsake you. St. Augustine has said that prayer is nothing but love. Prayer leads to a life of endless participation in the love that is God manifest.

Contemplation

1. Both Ramana Maharishi and St. Francis of Assisi advise us to surrender and to seek nothing -- absolutely nothing -- from God when we pray. The 12 Steps of AA ask us to pray only for God's will, not our own. Yet there seems to be a contradiction here -- an implied wanting or needing. After all, why would we pray to God if we didn't want something? Moreover, how can we recognize the will of God over our own self will? What are your thoughts on this dilemma?
2. The act of prayer has been described as a state of continual gratitude. What are you most grateful for?
3. The spiritual system of Taoism emphasizes aligning ourselves with nature, the natural way, God's will. The great Taoist

Master Lao Tzu challenges us: "Why not live your own life, not the life that others say you should?" Are you living your own life? If not, what would you do, or will you do, differently now?

Application

1. Sit down and construct your own prayer of gratitude or communion with God, or higher power.
2. Find some formal prayers from religious texts, such as the Prayer of Peace of St. Francis, the Pater Noster, The Serenity Prayer, the Gayatri Mantra, or the Hail Mary. As you pray, what feelings do you experience from these prayers?
3. Do you experience a difference in your inner state when offering prayers you have created, compared to when you are reciting already existing, well-known prayers? Which state is preferable to you?
4. For the next day, stop every hour on the hour for a brief one-minute formal or informal prayer. Become aware of how you feel the next day.

Lesson Nineteen

SPIRITUAL UNION

• • • • •

Illumination

"All creatures seek after unity: all multiplicity struggles towards it -- the universal name of all life is always this unity. All that flows outward is to flow backward into its source – God."

Johannes Tauler

A German mystic, Tauler, 1300-1361, was a preacher and theologian in the Dominican order. He was a student of Meister Eckhart. Known for his sermons, he taught that the state of the soul was affected more by a personal relationship with God than external practices.

Examination

Have you ever felt like a stranger or visitor on planet Earth? Do you feel like you just don't quite fit in here with the myriad of personal dramas, as well as strange values and ways of doing things? Perhaps you feel that you come from another planet or galaxy, where you might fit in better than you do here. As odd as these ideas may seem, there is a reason so many of us have them. It is because our true home, our true Kingdom, is not here on this planet, as Jesus so clearly pointed out ("My Kingdom is not of this world"). While residing physically on this earth, it is said that our higher Self, our multidimensional Self, also resides simultaneously in higher planes of consciousness. It is more than likely that when we become conscious of our existence in higher planes of consciousness, we are much more likely to feel at home, as if we truly live there.

Johannes Tauler's quote references God as the Source, or the Creator of, everything that is, was, and will be. That means that you and I come from God, and are manifestations of God's creative power. While we may appear to be two or more (the "many"), in reality we are One. Tauler indicates that we "seek Unity," which we interpret to mean that there is a felt lack in feeling different or other from who we truly are. As long as we do not experience ourselves as being in unison with the Source, we may always feel that something is awry, like a ship out of water. Finally, Tauler suggests that, just as our very existence is a manifestation of God's creative power, that same power which impelled us to move away from the Source – and incarnate on earth – will, eventually, drive us back to Source. Thus, our destiny, in a way, is already determined. We are going home! There is no other possibility.

Our fondest aspirations, laying deep in the recesses of our soul, essentially involve the return to our union with Source. Spiritual union, the joining of the lower self to God or higher power, is the penultimate goal of all spiritual programs. One cannot conceive of anything higher, purer, or more blissful in life. Moreover, spiritual union is our natural state. We can never be apart from God, even when it seems that we are far from home. The idea that we appear separate from God is an illusion, a distortion ('maya,' as the Hindus would say). As the great philosopher Ken Wilber has put it, the state of non-dual awareness, or unity consciousness, is that which "is always already." It is the very ground of our existence, as the Zen Buddhists put it, our own original nature. Yet, it exists right now, in this very moment.

The problem in life is that we are not aware of our unity; we are distracted; we put our attention outward, on all and everything but this seamless ground of unified awareness. Or, we believe that we will attain Unity Consciousness at some future time, when we are "better," or more well-prepared, students. These beliefs tend to delay our full recognition of the state of Unity Consciousness.

On my (Vincent's) spiritual journey, I am transforming my personal identity as a way of remembering who I am. Having been trained in childhood to view myself as a sinner with whom God has been displeased and has banished from heaven, I have been focused on perceiving my identity as one with the Divine. Shifting my identity from 'I am a sinner' to 'I am God' is a profound paradigm shift to say the least. This shift may appear to be the ultimate in ego gratification and narcissism. It is not. In changing my identity, I am not referring to changes in my personality, behavior (which, of course, is not always perfect), or a way of comparing myself to others. Instead, identifying with being the Self is more of an attunement, an awareness of who "I" am in the first place, and recognizing that every worldly identification regarding who I am (e.g., I am a writer, I am a therapist, etc.) is limiting, and potentially interfering with my ability to experience Unity Consciousness if I do not search further for who I am.

All spiritual techniques and strategies have, as their final goal, recapturing of and reintegration into the state of unity. All of the great mystics tell us that we are, in fact, indistinguishable in God. The great master Osho has said, "Only the same can do the same." That is, the divine in us recognizes the divine without, and merges back in the Source. Perhaps the most emphatic mystic was Meister Eckhart, who lived in Germany in the 1300s. He said, "God is my being, is my life, but if it is so, then what is God's must be mine, and what is mine God's. God's 'isness' is my 'isness,' and neither more nor less." Jewish Talmudic scholars taught that as God fills the world, the soul fills the body. Gandhi put it a bit differently, saying, "We may not be God, but we are of God, even as a little drop of water is of the ocean..." The small drop of water and ocean analogy constantly repeats throughout the mystical literature of all religious traditions. Man is likened to a tiny pool of water cut off from the vast ocean. This tiny pool of water eventually becomes stagnant; it loses its awareness that it is identical in nature with the water of the ocean. Until it awakens to its true nature and reunites with the vastness of the ocean, it will remain cut off and alienated.

In the great Vedic tradition in India, there is no mincing of words. "Aham Brahmasmi," is repeated, and it means 'I am Brahman.' 'I am the totality.' The jiva, or individual soul, is, in fact, a mirror image of Brahman, the All. Perhaps the great poet Ralph Waldo Emerson was the boldest in this regard. He said, "The simplest person who lovingly and with integrity worships God *becomes God...*" (italics mine). St. Francis de Sales has even told us that this realization can happen during our lifetime, not just after our death. To many, this may seem like blasphemy, the ultimate in egoism!! However, the union we are speaking of here is not the union of the ego and God; rather, it is the union of the soul with a higher power; it is the expansion of our consciousness to boundlessness.

There is, in fact, a solid and growing body of research on this developmental process, that we could call the development of consciousness or awareness. Psychologists and other scientists have found that it occurs in stages and is expressed in various states, moving from a state of disunion to the ultimate state of union. In Christianity, the stages often appear as purgation, illumination, and union. In Vedic psychology, the stages are transcendental consciousness, cosmic consciousness, God consciousness, and unity consciousness. Scientific research has found that an individual progresses unidirectionally through various stages of consciousness, increasing in clarity and eventually culminating in a permanent stage of union with God. In the Greek tradition, Plotinus said, "We can only apprehend God by entering a state in which you are your finite self no longer: in which the divine essence is communicated to you..." And the great psychiatrist Carl Jung has said that what truly matters is the infinite. He exhorts us to fix our attention on that and to avoid the futilities of lesser goals.

In his book *Power vs Force*, Dr. David Hawkins presents a scale of spiritual accomplishment, from the lowest state to the highest state. The scale is logarithmic, ranging from 1 (mere existence) to 1000 (the highest state of enlightenment). He does not claim that individuals progress on this scale in a unidirectional manner, but he does claim that there are substantial differences in abilities among persons in qualitatively different states of consciousness. For instance, an individual who generally vibrates at the level of 100 (fear) might approach a problematic situation using intimidation and force, whereas an individual who vibrates at the level of 500 (love) might deal with the same situation using the powers of loving kindness and benevolence.

Unity consciousness is universally seen as the great endpoint of human existence – Unio Mystica. When you engage in contemplative prayer and meditation, you contact, even if only transiently, the state of unity. As your meditation practice grows and your spiritual program solidifies, this experience gestates and germinates and grows on and on, until your ego dissipates and unboundedness and limitlessness prevail. Then, like a soaring Hawk returning to rest in its nest, you are home, and you are free...

It is said that each night as we sleep, our mind rests in the heart, in Unity Consciousness, but we are completely unaware of this experience. As we progress in spiritual attainment we are able to maintain complete conscious experience of the mind resting in the heart, and we develop the ability to consciously observe the mind resting in the heart not just during periods of dreaming, but in the waking state, dreaming state, and deep sleep state.

Contemplation

1. Have you ever had a unity experience such as losing yourself, forgetting yourself, and feeling at one, perhaps in nature or with someone you love? Describe that experience. Did it feel at all threatening?

2. We often feel so fragile and powerless as human beings. This makes it difficult to understand the wisdom of the mystics. Yet how do we reconcile the continual presence of references to unity that thread their way through all faiths at all times? Are these great spiritual individuals delusional? Are they lying to us? What do you think?
3. St. Augustine said, "Let me know myself, Lord, and I shall know thee." How would you interpret what he said?

Application

1. Take a walk in nature and reflect on the energy that pulses in every living thing you see. This energy can be seen by observing the ripples in water, feeling the wind on your face, seeing the moving clouds in the sky, and listening to the sounds of nature. Can you find that same energy within yourself?
2. Enter a church, temple, mosque, or other holy place, and be mindful of the effects of being in a sacred environment. You may notice the deafening sounds of silence, or feel the pull to have your attention drawn inward.
3. Think of the connections in your life, to your family, job, community, nature, your body, your mind, the deceased, and the earth. Notice how connected your body is to everything in this world. After contemplating this, ask yourself – can I really be disconnected from anything?
4. Get on the computer and Google Dr. John Haglin. He is a great quantum physicist and expert on consciousness. Visit his site and read about what quantum physics says about unity consciousness.

5. Japa (repetition of the name of God) is a form of meditation practiced in the East, particularly in India. Sit comfortably, and after a few minutes of silence, say to yourself – 'God and I are one' -- or – 'I am at one with God.' Allow your attention to gently settle between your eyebrows with your eyes closed. An alternative repetition is – 'Lord, come to me.' Say this in an easeful way, such that you are slowly imbibing and savoring these words. Allow space to have the words settle after you have said them. Practice this contemplative technique effortlessly for about 20 minutes.
6. As you lay in bed at night, waiting to fall asleep, pray to your favorite deity, to ask for blessings and teachings as you sleep, so that your time spent during the night is fruitful and productive.

Lesson Twenty

ON PEACE

• • • • •

Illumination

"Peace comes not from doing but from undoing: not from getting but from letting go..."

Satchidananda Saraswati

A highly renowned Indian spiritual teacher, Satchidananda, 1914-2002, wrote many books and gained some notoriety as the opening speaker at the Woodstock music festival. He was the founder of Integral Yoga and Yogaville in Buckingham, Virginia.

"After you have found inner peace, spiritual growth takes place harmoniously because you - now governed by the higher Self – will to do God's will, and do not need to be pushed into it."

Peace Pilgrim

Peace Pilgrim, 1908-1981, was an American nondenominational spiritual teacher, mystic, and activist. She walked across the United States many times, after experiencing a spiritual awakening following a long period of meditation.

Examination

Imagine that you never had a worry... about anything. Imagine your mind was always clear, free from any disturbance, like a cloudless blue sky. Further imagine that, although you might have this type of experience while in meditation, you also have this same experience when you are awake, with no effort, no matter what is happening at any moment, even while strolling down a crowded street in the middle of the city. This is an idea, however limited it may be, of the state of inner peace.

It seems counterintuitive to think of peace and tranquility as something we do not have to fight for, control, or get. We all want peace of mind, but it seems that only a few people have it naturally, or acquire it in life. And it appears that, throughout the history of humankind, we have had to go to war to maintain peace between countries, on a nearly continual basis. But is this true peace? Is it permanent? Is it unconditional? Can we ever get the mind to be in a state of peace?

Patanjali, who codified all of the various schools of yoga around the 5th century BCE, expounded his teachings in the book *The Yoga Sutras of Patanjali*. He tells us that there is really no peace of mind - only transcending the mind. When we transcend the mind, we open our being to the true Self, whose very nature is peace. Many of the great spiritual traditions agree that peace is best achieved through the practice of meditation and contemplation. Peace exists within us if we will just search for it. Within each of us there is a center in the middle of the cyclone of worldly events, a place of calm. We are invited to take up residency there.

Peace has always been elevated to a high status in writings of religion and spirituality. In the Old Testament (Isaiah 9:6), the Messiah is referred to as the "Prince of Peace." The Hebrew greeting 'Shalom' means peace, but appears to refer to a state of completeness or wholeness, and not just a cessation of war or dispute. In Sanskrit, the word for peace, "Shanti," is commonly used at the beginning and end of prayers, signifying calmness, tranquility, or bliss. In the Roman Catholic Mass, "peace" is accorded a high place of significance, as immediately prior to receiving and distributing Holy Communion (the body of Christ), the priest recites the words from Lord Jesus: "I leave you peace, my peace I give you."

The great spiritual Masters insist that to attain peace there is really nothing to do, but much to undo. We need to decondition our minds (our ego sense), letting go of all the negative conditioning and the stressors that have accumulated in our lives. In other words, much of what we have learned needs to be unlearned. But we cannot force these conditioned habits and incorrect knowledge out of our minds. Instead, through spiritual practices, we transcend the mind. As we gently detach from the habit of thinking – usually about negative, painful, and worrisome thoughts – we gradually learn to abide in a state of peace. When we let go, great qualities such as compassion, friendliness, and bliss automatically and naturally manifest.

When there is peace, there is complete acceptance of how things are, rather than an insistence that things 'should be different,' or 'need to be fixed.' The developer of the psychotherapeutic method Rational Emotive Therapy (RET), Dr. Albert Ellis, preached that when we insist upon how things "should be" rather than embracing how "things are," we wind up living a "shouldy kind of life." We are filled with anxieties, resentments, and anger that things are not as we understand, and expect they should be. We will not attain peace until we can embrace the present as it is, by letting go of all of our preconceived beliefs about how things 'should' be. Essentially, peace is attained as we surrender completely to the will of God, understanding that it is God who does and accomplishes everything. Surrendering to God's will at this point in the 21-step course has a different quality than it likely had earlier.

At this point of the course, surrender to God's will comes with the deep feeling that this is also surrender to our will. We gain a growing sense that our will is merging and aligning with God's will. Following God's will is completely consistent with our goals for ourselves and others. Here is an example from my experience. There have been a number of occasions when I am listening to TV or radio and am aware that my inner being prefers to be in a more meditative and peaceful state. I find myself turning off the electronics and entering a quiet, internal state. At these times, I feel like I am making no sacrifice at all.

Another steppingstone on the path to peace is, in the words of the 20th century sage, Peace Pilgrim, to relinquish the feelings of separateness. This requires the viewpoint that all of us are cells in the body of humanity (what Catholics may refer to as the 'Mystical Body of Christ'). Thus, we are not separate from our fellow humans. Instead, in a very real sense, we all are part of a totality, or what some current scientists are now calling 'the unified field,' or what has been referred to as collective consciousness.

Peace exists in the realization that we are indeed 'one,' not two or more. To obtain the state of peace, it is necessary to experience that we each are truly brothers and sisters in one holy family. On the David Hawkins scale, the energy level of peace vibrates at 600, on the scale of 1-1000. He notes that in this state, the distinction between subject and object disappears. In other words, the observer merges with the observed, in an experience of bliss. Peace Pilgrim described her experience of peace in this manner: "I felt a oneness – oneness with all my fellow human beings, oneness with all of creation. I have never felt really separate since" (from www.peacepilgrim.com).

With this realization, we can become very excited about the fact that we have a definite role to play in creating peace on earth! As we experience the state of peace that comes from spiritual practices, such as meditation, we create not only an internal peace; we also assist in creating peace within others, and within all of manifest creation. The implications of this idea are immense. The idea that meditators create a peace not only within themselves, but within the world at large, is truly revolutionary. Many years ago, Maharishi Mahesh Yogi predicted that only a small number of meditators participating in a Transcendental Meditation program could produce a measurable improvement in the amount of peace and harmony in a geographic area. This was called the 'Super Radiance Effect' (a term borrowed from Physics), which is essentially a statement about action at a distance. Since Maharishi made this statement, there have been over 49 published research studies on this effect. (There are a number of research scientists affiliated with TM which allowed Maharishi to collect data in support of his contentions.) Variables assessed in these studies include engagements in armed conflict, crime rates, violent fatalities (homicides, suicides, and motor vehicle fatalities), economic indicators, and broad quality of life indices. The effects of meditation on other variables, such as rates of diseases, hospital admissions, infant mortality, divorce, cigarette and alcohol consumption, and GNP (see www.TruthAboutTM.com by Dr. David Orme-Johnson) have been investigated as well.

In 1993, a group of 4000 TM meditators in Washington, DC, carried out a scientific demonstration during the summer. After meditating up to four hours per day for seven weeks, it was estimated that violent crime was reduced by 23%. The Chief of Police claimed before the onset of the study that only a storm dumping 20 inches of snow could reduce crime to that great an extent. Clearly the Chief of Police was not anticipating such a striking reduction in the crime rate simply by having a number of people sit on the lawns to meditate.

More recently, Davies and Alexander (2005) reported on the effects of participation in one or more of seven, group meditation programs (World Peace Assemblies) held during a two-year period in the Lebanon War. The results showed reductions in the numbers of war fatalities and increases in the use of methods involving cooperation and conflict resolution following each of the group meditation programs. The effectiveness of the intervention was attributed to a reduction of tension in the unified field of consciousness among the warring nations; or, more simply, a reduction of their collective stress.

The obstacles to peace are mental, and include all negative thoughts and feelings. The science of yoga informs us that thinking disturbs our inner peace, and, at the same time, perhaps the peace of the collective field of individuals. This is why the practice of meditation is so important. During meditation, we transcend thoughts. We neither entertain them nor reject them. We assume a 'not minding' attitude toward them. As we meditate, we improve not only our individual wellbeing, but also the collective wellbeing of a town or city or country. Thus, when we meditate or pray, we do it for ourselves and for others. In times of tragedy, such as the recent slayings in a bar in Orlando, FL, meditation and prayer can reduce the stress for all of the individuals affected in the unified field.

The nature of the Self is bliss (ananda). When we rest in the Higher Self, we realize that we have nothing to prove and nothing to strive for. Peace seeks nothing outside of itself -- it is not a means to an end. Peace is the end. Peace comes through being, not having. It is our true and natural state.

Contemplation

1. Schopenhauer, the great philosopher, tells us we must abandon all pretense to gain peace. What pretenses do you have and why do you think you have them?
2. Einstein said that peace comes from understanding- not by force. What areas of your life do you need to understand more? Can you see how peace would naturally arise if you acquired more understanding?
3. Satchidananda has emphasized the importance of letting go -- doing nothing, surrendering, and accepting. What do you think his rationale is for saying this? Can you think of any instances in your life when you stopped fighting something and let things happen -- did it bring you any measure of peace?

APPLICATION.

1. Let go of some inner struggle -- drop it like a hot potato! Do you experience a sense of peace?
2. St. Francis DeSales tells us to hang on to what inner peace we have, and do everything we can to keep it. Practice that over the next 24 hours. Resolve not to let anything take away your inner peace.
3. The 14th century Italian scholar Petrarch tells us to identify the enemies of peace, including anger, greed, pride, and ambition, and banish them from our lives. Over the next 24 hours, identify one of your enemies to peace, and do what you can to banish it from your life.
4. Spend some time sitting quietly by a river or a stream. Close your eyes and listen to the sound. Allow your being to merge with the sound, such that you experience yourself as the sound. Or you could sit by a hill or mountain. Observe its state of stillness and quietude, close your eyes, and experience the same stillness within your being.
5. Sound, or mantra, is one of the most effective methods we know of inducing a meditative state. In this meditation, we will practice easefully and effortlessly. Begin by sitting quietly, upright in a chair or on the floor with your back against a wall or door for about two minutes. Notice that your mind is constantly thinking, and there is no effort to this thought -- it just comes and goes on its own. In the same effortless way, now introduce a mantra, and begin to think it and repeat it internally. Our mantra is: "Om Shanti" – pronounced ...**Aumm Shantee...** allow yourself to slowly repeat this mantra**...** just innocently be with it... if you find yourself straying away from

a mantra, calmly come back to it. Most importantly, do not try to resist any thoughts, feelings, or sensations that you have during meditation -- just let them come. Likewise, do not resist any external sounds you hear -- just let them come and go on their own. Practice for about 15 minutes. When you think that time is up, gently open your eyes and look at the clock to confirm this. If you have more time to go, return to meditation -- if you are finished, sit quietly for about a minute, slowly open your eyes, and resume activity.

Lesson Twenty-One

LOVING SERVICE

• • • • •

Illumination

"I slept and dreamt that life was joy. I awoke and found that life was service. I acted and behold, service was joy ..."

Rabindranath Tagore

Tagore, 1861- 1941, was a Bengali poet of India, who was a great influence on Indian art, literature, and music. He was the first non-Europeans to win the Nobel Prize in Literature in 1913.

Examination

As the 12-Steps of Alcoholics Anonymous reminds us, it's not enough to "make it" only to fulfill our individual needs. Oh, sure, it's great to become free, to wake up, to achieve self-mastery and self-integration. But we live in a world with others, and they are suffering, too. And as long as they suffer, so do we. On this earth, we are interconnected, which means that we rise and fall together. When any one of us is lifted up, we are all lifted up. So we reach out to help others and, in so doing, we ourselves reach the highest heights.

Why do we do this? We do not perform service to become greater. We are already great, Divine Beings of Light. We perform service to live in the constant awareness of who we really are. We seek to experience the Bliss of the Self, or God's Love in all actions, in every sentient being and every insentient object everywhere we look. When we begin to become spiritually free and achieve higher states of consciousness, we begin to "see the Self in all beings, and all beings in the Self." As you grow spiritually, you indeed come to the realization that there is one Self, one being, and that we are all individualized expressions of it. As we mature spiritually, we naturally desire to reach out and help others because as they are, so we are. So we give to others, we offer service to others. And we benefit through conscious participation in the processes of love and creation. It is the Tao, or the way of things.

It has been said that service is God's love in action. As we become filled with God's love and come to know God more intimately, we become a vehicle for his love. And service to others is a concrete manifestation of this love. The great saint Satya Sai Baba has said that we should serve man because God has no need of service. The great physicist Albert Einstein said, "It is plain that we exist for our fellow man." Service to others is a crucial developmental milestone or step on the path to spiritual maturity. And there are many ways we can demonstrate service, from the smallest, simplest gesture of kindness to the most selfless philanthropic career.

Many of us become so caught up in our own lives that we forget about others. We become pressed for time. We get so caught up in the drama of our lives that we forget about the needs of others. Perhaps we might feel that we have little to offer others because of the stresses in our own lives -- we are barely making it, so how can we help anyone else?

We may not feel we have the energy or the resources to be of service to anyone in this world. We can relax in the knowledge that there are many ways to be of service to others and of service to God. The great Indian Saint Ramana Maharishi tells us that the best way to be of service to others is to make our minds up to be tranquil. Once we obtain a calming presence, everyone we meet will become automatically affected by our purity and clarity, and they will be able to experience their own inner stillness. So we take care of ourselves, we purify our mind and body, and become mirrors of the Divine.

In this way we do not have to exert effort in being of service to others -- just our 'being there' puts us at service. The Vietnamese Buddhist Monk, Thich Nhat Hahn, discussed one means of offering service in an interview with Oprah Winfrey (available on YouTube) when he stated that he has four mantras. The first is "Darling, I am here for you." The meaning of this mantra, he explains, is that when you love someone, you offer your presence; you are fully available to listen to them and be with them. You ease the suffering of others purely by being with them in their time of need. Anyone who has ever been in the company of a holy man or woman intuitively understands the state of peace emanating from his/her being. We simply want to be with them, and just being in their company elevates our lives. Radiating waves of peace, love, and stillness is truly a great service. You can be the same way with others, and you probably already are with some of the people in your life.

Saint Therese of Lisieux ("The Little Flower"), a 19th century saint, wrote, "What matters in life is not great deeds, but great love." Like Mother Teresa of Calcutta from the 20th century, Saint Therese focused on doing the smallest of tasks with love. This is the essence of service. Opening a door, offering a smile or a flower, waving at someone, or giving a compassionate glance are effective ways of being of service to others, perhaps not only to those persons we know well, but to persons we do not know very well.

> ... the best way to be of service to others is to make our minds up to be tranquil.
>
> *Ramana Maharishi*

Actions performed with love and joy are 'service' to the world, particularly if there is no desire for personal reward, but simply a desire to perform an action for its own sake, while seeing God's creation in everything you do.

When we speak of service, we do not advocate giving away everything we have and becoming poor. There is no value in becoming poor, per se, unless it is to serve as an example to others, or live completely free of all worldly entanglements. We give within our means, using discrimination. After all, we are the Self as much as any 'other' person is the Self. When we give, it may be the gift of time, work, money, love, or good wishes.

Offering service is not about self-deprivation or martyrdom. It is not about putting ourselves on 'pedestals,' as people who give extensively and never take anything from anyone else. This type of giving can be just another 'ego trip,' a way of enhancing our sense of self-importance.

In this regard, it is essential to understand that not only is giving to others a great service, but so is the willingness to receive from others. In a very real way, receiving is as important as giving in maintaining the continuous cycle of love and positive energy in the world. Many of us are well-trained in being givers, but we do not give others the opportunity to show their love for us through their actions and gifts. Refusing to allow others the opportunity to give to us can sever the flow of love between people. When we allow others to nurture us or give to us, we allow them an opportunity to experience God's love. In this way, we participate in the cycle of giving and receiving, almost unaware or unconcerned about the difference between them.

When you offer some simple good works that benefit others, you further magnify, amplify, and purify your own awareness, which gives you a still greater capacity to be of service to others. In other words, the more you give, the more capacity you have to give, and the more joy you experience in giving to others. This truth is expressed well in this segment of the St. Francis Prayer... "O, Divine Master, it is in giving that we receive." As you serve others, you become glorified; as your consciousness expands, your intimacy deepens, and you quickly achieve the goal of your spiritual path. Anyone, regardless of skill, money, resources, or intellect, can serve with love, and when you help others, you have the power of the universe behind you. And this great universal power frees up your own inner power, to expand to its own boundlessness. This is the great joy of which Tagore speaks.

Service is embodied through the life of the contemporary saint Mata Amritanandamayi ("Amma"), also affectionately known as 'The Hugging Saint.' She has travelled the world for many years, greeting individuals with hugs while showering them with her love. To date she has hugged over 34 million people. A visit to her website (www.amma.org) indicates her boundless, global humanitarian service projects, spread over 40 countries. Amma began giving away food and possessions as a young girl and has not stopped since. Her indefatigable energy, evident when one meets her, is a concrete example of the power of love in action.

Pay attention to the slightest bit of loving service you give to the world. Scriptures say you will be repaid a thousand fold.

Contemplation

1. Confucius said, he who wishes to secure the good of others has already secured his own. The motive, the intention, matters. As you look at your own life, examine the motives behind your charitable works.
2. Horace Mann has said, "Doing nothing for others is the undoing of ourselves." We understand this quote to mean that when we hoard goods and resources for ourselves without giving to others, we block the flow of grace in our lives, and we slowly become depleted of our wealth, especially our loving presence. Think of your own experiences giving to and assisting others. How did it make you feel? How did it change you?
3. When you read spiritual literature, you might be struck by the number of enlightened sages who say that you should achieve the Higher Self, and this is the most effective way to help others. Yet sitting in prolonged meditation and prayer has been criticized as self-absorption, narcissistic withdrawal, or solitary detachment. Do you believe this? How do you think

spiritual practices can help others, and why do you think that the great enlightened ones are so strong on this point?

4. This is a simple meditation which highlights you becoming aware of the other. We will start with the awareness of inanimate creation. With this exercise we develop an attitude of reverence and respect for all of creation, for all of the objects around us, as they are all creations of God.

   Go outside and pick up an object, such as a leaf, a stone, or a piece of wood. Let the object rest in the palm of your outstretched hand... close your eyes and simply feel the object in your hand... become as fully aware of it as possible, feel the sensation it produces... now explore it with your fingers, and do so gently and reverently... feel its roughness or smoothness, its weight, its temperature... and now touch it to other parts of your body, and notice the differences... after you become aware of it with your sense of touch, open your eyes, and look at all the details of it: its color, its form, and shape... now gently place the object in your lap and speak to it... ask it about its life, its origins, its future, where it came from... now realize that this object was created by God; that it is a part of Her, and that both you and this object are bathed in God's awareness... feel the connectedness of all things, to all of creation, to other human beings... notice any changes in feelings or attitude towards the object... and lovingly return it to its place.

Application

1. Over 19 research studies show that the practice of meditation cleanses the social environment, reducing stress, improving

health, and reducing chaos. Sit down and meditate for about 30 minutes and then notice any of its effects in the environment around you, or in your interactions with others.

2. Give of yourself in some small way over the next 24 hours. For this exercise, perform an action that is designed to help someone, but does not involve giving money. It is preferable if the action involves your interacting with another person. Notice its effects on your feelings, thoughts, and mood.
3. Talk to someone who performs service, as a job or profession, or as a volunteer. Note how this individual benefits from activities involving service.
4. Sit down and put together a simple daily plan of doing at least one gesture of service to others.
5. Next time someone gives you a gift, accept it as fully and joyfully as possible. Let the other person know that you are happy to receive the gift. Focus on the act of 'receiving' and resist the feeling to repay or feel indebted to the other person. Give the other person the 'gift' or your gratitude and appreciation in receiving a gift.

THE LAST LESSON

WHY?

• • • • •

ILLUMINATION

"The most strongly enforced of all known taboos is the taboo against knowing who or what you really are, behind the mask of your apparently separate, independent, and isolated ego."

Alan Watts.

Alan Watts, 1915-1973, was a British philosopher, theologian, and Episcopal priest, who wrote over 25 books and articles on Eastern and Western religion.

EXAMINATION

You have studied and practiced exercises from 21 different spiritual lessons. In all likelihood something significant about you has changed. Your relationship to yourself, to 'so-called' others, to the world, and to God is likely not the same as before you started. At this point, however, you must have confronted one nagging question over and over: why is all of this study and work necessary?

If who we are is a manifestation of the Divine, if we are no one and nothing other than God, and if what is going on is simply God searching for Him/Herself, why has God gone through the trouble to do this? And, furthermore, why is life on earth often one big struggle?

What we have presented is that there is no achieving or attaining anything when it comes to spirituality. The great quest for union with God is based on eliminating ignorance of the true nature of existence. It has been likened to cleaning a foggy glass. The search for God implies that the divine lies somewhere outside ourselves, and that could never be true, for we are, as the great Integral philosopher Ken Wilber has put it- always already spirit. There is no place to go when it comes to spiritual matters. There is only a waking up to that which already exists. And the desire or impulse to seek God or spiritual liberation is the very impulse which blocks that very realization, for it is based on the faulty idea that God is not omnipresent. **We simply cannot find tomorrow that which already exists in the eternal now**. Thus, the spiritual quest is a journey from here.... to here. This is a journey in which we 'wake up.' We do not go anywhere, per se.

The final lesson in spirituality is to realize that we never left where we aspire to go. We never lost what we deign to achieve. In this sense, the eternal spiritual quest is a denial of reality itself. Yet, paradoxically, it is a journey well worth taking, for it leads to its own extinction, and to the state of **unity.** We simply cannot abandon the spiritual search. We are kidding ourselves if we give up and abandon God, for we cannot pretend we are other than what we are -- not taking up the great spiritual journey is tantamount to taking it! Both are equally fruitless. But the latter is essential.

As David's spiritual mentor always said, "You have everything you need for enlightenment right now." Right here, right now, in the eternal present, you are always already pure spirit, the Self. There is nothing outside yourself—there is nothing *but* Self—you do not exist in the world; the world exists in you, and the world is not separate from you. You have never been out of your own original, unified state, so you can never strive to reenter it!! As the Upanishads tells us, "The seeker is the sought." We cannot search for ourselves because we all **are** ourselves.

So all of these teachings lead to two profound questions: why don't we intuitively realize the truth of our own nature, and why did God create this illusion, this apparent belief that we are human beings with failings, rather than the Source of all, in the first place?

To the rational, logical, conscious mind, there is no answer that will satisfy. We (mostly) agree that there is no justice in the world (bad things happen to good people, only the good die young) and that the world seems just a little crazier or more disorderly every day.

Eastern philosophy and religion, particularly the philosophy of Vedanta, attempts to address these questions. The answer given is that all of the creation of which we are aware is nothing but a Divine play or a Divine joke, if you will, and we are the actors. Numerous spiritual masters and scriptures have discussed this at some length.

The philosopher Alan Watts, author of numerous books and articles about Christianity and Zen Buddhism, emphasized that the phenomenal world is simply the Great Self, playing a game of hide-and-seek. The above quotation, taken from p. 11 of his publication '*The Book: On the Taboo Against Knowing Who You Are*,' describes not only this viewpoint, taken from Vedanta (ancient Hindu scriptures), but also emphasizes that all of humanity is complicit in hiding our truth from ourselves. He states that "We suffer from a hallucination, from a false and distorted sensation of our own existence as human organisms" (p. 8).

Why does God play this game of hide-and-seek? To answer this question, we might turn to our own experience as human beings. Most likely you have watched a mother play a game of Peek-A-Boo with her infant. Both mother and infant love this game, and can play for a long time. This game is entertaining, provided that the infant has not developed the concept of 'object permanence,' which is the understanding that objects continue to maintain their existence even after they are hidden from view. Infants develop full understanding of object permanence around 12 months of age.

Peek-A-Boo is great fun for the infant who appears to truly 'believe' that her mother has disappeared when she places a towel or blanket over her. At that moment, the infant appears to act as if the mother has disappeared. But, moments later, when the mother removes the barrier between herself and the baby, the infant squeals with delight! He has rediscovered his mother. She is ALIVE! Perhaps the most fascinating aspect of this game is that the mother can repeat this sequence again and again in a span of a few minutes, and her baby will react as if she is playing and discovering her mother anew each and every time. Imagine yourself in the infant's position. She is convinced her mother has disappeared when she is hidden – a distressing experience to say the least – but then is jubilant the moment she again discovers that her mother still exists!

Can this be the experience God is seeking? To play the game of pretending to be other than She is, which causes sadness, and then to experience the jubilation of re-experiencing Herself in all Her fullness!

The game of Peek-A-Boo is joyful is because the mother exists all along! She never really left the infant.

The great spiritual traditions tell us that our current dilemma is brought about by the fact that we are resisting, and avoiding accepting our eternal, unbounded state of pure spirit. For some reason, we run away from the truth, and we cannot allow ourselves to simply rest in omnipresent spirit. In this sense, we play a game with ourselves, pretending to be something that we are not. One day, however, we tire of the game. We grow weary of our own bondage, and we strike out on the spiritual path. And, as we move through the stages, states, and phases of spiritual development, from time to time we get a glimpse of our original nature and we realize that we have arrived. However, our nervous systems usually cannot sustain this realization, and it fades. So we go back to spiritual practices, and again make our way on the spiritual path. Until, one day, the game is up! We drop our avoidance and simply rest in ever-present, unified awareness. And this state of affairs can come about literally at any moment in our lives -- the eternal truth infuses itself into the temporal. We fall into unity, and our long trek ceases.

The great eternal quest on the spiritual path is the *pathless* path to the gateless gate, the illusionary journey we are all destined to take. So we go on reading spiritual literature. We go on praying and meditating. We go on contemplating. We go on providing service to others and nurturance to ourselves. We go on the studying the great spiritual traditions and the enlightened individuals who came before us. And we are secure in the guarantee that our consciousness, little by little, will purify, and we will radiate in pure being, as we always already have...

THE END

Application

Listen to the song "The Mountain" by Donovan. Understand in your own words the meaning of the refrain: "First there is a mountain, then there is no mountain, then there is."

REFERENCES

• • • • •

Alexander, Eben (2012). *Proof of Heaven.* New York, NY: Simon and Shuster.

Aurobindo, Sri (1984). *The Mother.* Pondicherry, India: Sri Aurobindo Ashram.

Campbell, Polly (2012). *How to Reach Enlightenment.* London,England: Hodder Education.

Chandwani, K.D., Perkins,G., Nagendra, H.R., Raghuram, N.V, Spelman, A., Nagarathna, R., Johnson, K., Fortier, A., Arun, B., Wei, Q., Haddad, R., Morris, G.S., Scheetz, J., Chaoul, A., Cohen, L. Randomized, Controlled Trial of Yoga in Women with Breast Cancer Undergoing Radiotherapy. *Journal of Clinical Oncology*, April 2014, Vol. 32, Issue 10,1058-1065.

Chodron, Pema (2013). *How to Meditate: A Practical Guide to Making Friends with Your Mind.* Boulder, CO: Sounds True.

Cope, Stephen (1999). *Yoga and the Quest for the True Self.* New York, NY: Bantam Books.

Davies, J. L. and C. N. Alexander. Alleviating political violence through reducing collective tension: Impact Assessment analysis of the Lebanon war. *Journal of Social Behavior and Personality*, 2005, 17: 285-338.

Dalai Lama, HH. (2009). *Becoming Enlightened.* New York, NY: Atria Press.

Ellison, Christopher G., Matt Bradshaw, Kevin J. Flannelly, and Kathleen C. Galek. (2014) Prayer, Attachment to God, and Symptoms of Anxiety-Related Disorders among US Adults. *Sociology of Religion* 75: 208-233.

Frazier, Jan (2012). *The Freedom of Being: At Ease with What Is.* San Francisco, CA: Weiser Books.

Frazier, Jan (2007) *When Fear Falls Away: The Story of a Sudden Awakening*. San Francisco, CA: Weiser Books.

Frazier, Vidya (2002). *The Art of Letting Go: A Pathway to Inner Freedom*. Nevada City, CA: Blue Dolphin Press.

Godman, David (1986). *No Mind, I am the Self*: The Lives and Teachings of Sri Lakshmana Swami and Mathru Sri Sarada. Banumathy Ramanandham Sri Lakshmana Ashram.

Hariharananda Aranya, Swami(1983). *Yoga Philosophy of Patanjali*. Albany: NY State University of New York Press.

Hawkins, David (2004). *Power versus Force*. West Sedona, AZ: Veritas.

Kabat-Zinn, J (1994). *Wherever You Go There You Are: Mindfulness Meditation in Everyday Life*. NY: New York Hyperion.

Kempton, Sally (2011). *Meditation for the Love of It: Enjoying Your Own Deepest Experience*. Sounds True.

John of the Cross, Saint (1953). *Dark Night of the Soul*. The Newman Press, Westminster, Maryland.

Koenig, Harold, G. *Religion, spirituality, and health: a review and update. Advances in Mind-body Medicine,* 2015, 29 (3): 19-26.

Kripananda, Swami (1995). *The Sacred Power: A Seeker's Guide to Kundalini*. South Fallsburg, NY: The SYDA Foundation.

Long, Jeffrey & Perry, Paul (2010). *Evidence of the Afterlife.* New York, NY: Harper One.

Lazar, Sara, W. *Mindfulness practice leads to increases in regional brain grey matter density. Psychiatry Research,* 2011, 191 (1), 36-43.

Maa, Sai (2013). *Petals of Grace: Essential Teachings for Self-Mastery. United States of America,Sai Maa, LLC*

Mata Amritanandamayi (May 2012). *Make Humility A Habit.* Matruvani. M.A. Mission Trust, Kerala, India. Vol. 23, No. 9, p 2-5

Muktananda, Swami (1974). *Getting Rid of What You Haven't Got.* Oakland, CA: The SYDA Foundation.

Muktananda, Swami (1985). *Does Death Really Exist?* Gurudev Siddha Peeth, Ganeshpuri, India: The SYDA Foundation.

Newberg, Andrew & Waldman, M.R. (2016) *How Enlightenment Changes Your Brain.* New York, NY: Avery (an imprint of Penguin Random House).

O'Connell, D.F. & Bevinno, D. L. (2015). *Prescribing Health: Transcendental Meditation in Contemporary Medical Care.* Lanham, Maryland: Rowan and Littlefield.

Reiner, K., Tibi, L., & Lipsitz, J.D. (2013) Do mindfulness-based interventions reduce pain intensity? A critical review of the literature. *Pain Medicine, Issue 14, Vol. 2, pp 230-242.*

Ricard, Matthieu (2010). *Why Meditate? Working with Thoughts and Emotions.* New York, NY: Hay House.

Seppala, E.M.,Nitschke, J.B., Tudorascu, D.L., Hayes, A., Goldstein, M.R., Nguyen, D.T.H., Perlman, D. & Davidson, R.J. (2014). Breathing-based meditation decreases posttraumatic stress disorder symptoms in military veterans: A randomized controlled longitudinal study. *Journal of Traumatic Stress*, Vol.27, No. 4, pp 397-405.

Sogyal Rinpoche (1993). *The Tibetian Book of Living and Dying.* Rigpa New York, NY: Harper Collins.

Sivananda, Swami (1985) What *Becomes of the Soul After Death*? Dist. Tehri-Garhwal, U.P. Himalayas, India: The Divine Life Society.

Sperry, L. and Shafranske, E.P. (2005) *Spiritually Oriented Psychotherapy*. Washington, DC: The American Psychological Association.

Taylor, Jill Bolte (2008). *My Stroke of Insight*. New York, NY: Viking Press.

Tolle, Eckhart (1999). The *Power of Now*. Novato, CA: New World Library.

Toussaint, L, Shields, G.S., Dorn, G. & Slavich, G.M. (2016) Effects of lifetime stress exposure on mental and physical health in young adulthood: How stress degrades and forgiveness protects health. *Journal of Health Psychology*, Vol. 21 (6), 1004-1014.

Waltman, M.A., Russell, D.C., Coyle, C.T., Enright, R.D., Holter, A.C., & Swoboda, C.M. (2009). The effects of a forgiveness intervention on patients with coronary artery disease. *Psychology and Health,* Vol. 24, Issue 1, p. 11-27.

Watts, Alan (1972). *The Book: On the Taboo Against Knowing Who You Are*. New York, NY: Vintage Books.

Wilber, Ken (2003). *Kosmic Consciousness*. Audio CD. Sounds True.

Van Der Kolk, Bessel (2014). The Body Keeps the Score: Brain, Mind, and Body in the Healing of Trauma. New York, NY: Viking Press.

Yogananda, Paramanhansa (2009). *The Essence of Self-Realization.* Nevada City, CA: Crystal Clarity Publishers.

AUTHOR BIOS

• • • • •

Dr. Vincent Morello received a doctorate in Human Development from the Pennsylvania State University in 1983 and a master's degree in Psychology from West Virginia University. He works as a licensed psychologist at Wayne Counseling Center in Wayne, PA and has over 30 years of experience. He has trained doctoral Psychology students and Family Practice residents in addition to teaching numerous undergraduate psychology courses. He has published in psychology journals, magazines, and online newsletters. Since 1982, he has been a student of a number of enlightened Yoga Masters.

Dr. David O'Connell is the author of seven books in the areas of psychology, addictions, and spirituality. He is a licensed psychologist in Pennsylvania and New Mexico with 35 years of clinical and academic experience. He has been practicing Meditation for 40 years. Recently, he compiled the edited volume, **Prescribing Health: Transcendental Meditation in Contemporary Medical**

Care with Deborah Bevvino, Ph.D.. Dr. O'Connell specializes in forensics, neuropsychological testing, and medical psychology. He received his doctorate from Temple University in 1986, and his master's degree from Loyola University, Baltimore, MD in 1978. He is a board certified forensic psychologist at the American College of Forensic Examiners International, and is a member of the American Board of Medical Psychology

Lightning Source UK Ltd.
Milton Keynes UK
UKHW020653220820
368653UK00007B/190